EDUCATION

Launching a Redesign of University Principal Preparation Programs

Partners Collaborate for Change

Elaine Lin Wang, Susan M. Gates, Rebecca Herman, Monica Mean, Rachel Perera, Tiffany Tsai, Katie Whipkey, Megan Andrew

For more information on this publication, visit www.rand.org/t/RR2612

Library of Congress Cataloging-in-Publication Data is available for this publication.
ISBN: 978-1-9774-0159-5

Published by the RAND Corporation, Santa Monica, Calif.
© Copyright 2018 RAND Corporation
RAND® is a registered trademark.

Support RAND
Make a tax-deductible charitable contribution at
www.rand.org/giving/contribute

www.rand.org

Preface

As part of its deep commitment to improving school leadership, The Wallace Foundation launched the University Principal Preparation Initiative (UPPI) in July 2016. The four-year, $48.5 million initiative supports seven universities, their district and state partners, and mentor programs to redesign the universities' principal preparation programs according to evidence-based principles and practices. RAND Corporation researchers are analyzing the implementation of the initiative and changes in the design and delivery of the principal preparation program. A UPPI goal is to generate lessons that other university principal preparation programs and their partners can adopt or adapt as they undertake their own principal preparation system improvement efforts. To this end, research and reporting on UPPI focuses on cross-site themes rather than on documenting the details of change at each site.

This report provides insight into the first year of UPPI implementation. It will be of particular interest to universities seeking to elevate the quality of their principal preparation programs in evidence-based ways, to districts looking to play an influential role in shaping school leader preparation, and to state education agencies around the country looking for potential levers to support such work. Following the full report on early implementation, we are planning to release in fall 2020 a report focused on the intersection of UPPI and state reform efforts. The final report on UPPI implementation and changes in candidates' experience is scheduled for publication in 2022.

This study was undertaken by RAND Education, a unit of the RAND Corporation that conducts research on prekindergarten, kindergarten through grade 12 (K–12), and higher education issues, such as assessment and accountability, choice-based and standards-based school reform, vocational training, and the value of arts education and policy in sustaining and promoting well-rounded communities. This research was sponsored by The Wallace Foundation. The Wallace Foundation is committed to improving learning and enrichment for disadvantaged children, with a focus on school leadership, afterschool and summer learning, arts education, and social emotional learning, as well as improving the vitality of the arts for everyone.

More information about RAND can be found at www.rand.org. Questions about this report should be directed to Elaine Lin Wang at ewang@rand.org, and questions about RAND Education should be directed to edandlabormgmt@rand.org.

Contents

Figures, Tables, and Boxes

Figures

Tables

Boxes

Summary

School principals play a significant role in today's public schools (Grissom and Loeb, 2011; Harvey and Holland, 2013; Knapp et al., 2010; Louis et al., 2010). They are charged with complex responsibilities that can include developing a school vision and culture, supporting teacher effectiveness, managing challenges and crises, communicating with the greater community, and more. At the turn of the millennium, however, many public schools faced a crisis in school leadership marked by high turnover, difficulties in finding replacements for departing principals, and a perception that newly hired principals lacked the skills to succeed in their positions (Gates et al., 2003). School district leaders, principals, and preparation program representatives themselves perceived university preparation programs as underperforming in their training of future school leaders (Bottoms and O'Neill, 2001; Briggs et al., 2013; Manna, 2015). A vast majority of superintendents surveyed on this topic in 2016 thought that program improvements were necessary (Davis, 2016). These district leaders rated the level of preparation as "less than effective" on the full set of common school leader competencies, such as recruiting and selecting teachers. Principals themselves were also critical of their preparation, with about half of principals surveyed rating their programs as poor to fair in preparing them to deal with diverse school environments and in-school policies (Davis, 2016). In a 2005 study by Levine, 89 percent of principals surveyed said that their program did not prepare graduates to cope with classroom realities. Perhaps most surprisingly, a fair number of program representatives agreed with this assessment: Davis (2016) reports that more than one-third of program representatives reported that their existing programs did not prepare graduates well.

The limited existing research on university-based principal preparation programs suggests that key features that make such programs successful are lacking. These program features include an emphasis on leadership skills with a demonstrated relationship to student and school success, comprehensive clinical experiences that are linked to coursework, high-quality supervision of clinical experiences, and selective admission into the program (Davis, 2016; Fry, Bottoms, and O'Neill, 2005; Hess and Kelly, 2007; Sherman and Cunningham, 2006). These and additional evidence-based features and contexts of effective university principal preparation programs are presented in brief in Table S.1.

Table S.1
Evidence-Based Features and Contexts of Successful University Principal Preparation Programs

Feature or Context	Description
Program features	
Coherent curriculum	The program's course of study is focused on instruction and school improvement, integrating theory and practice through active learning and input from faculty with experience in school administration.
Supervised clinical experiences	The program provides opportunities for participants to engage in leadership activities over a long period of time and obtain constructive feedback from effective principals.
Active recruiting	The program searches for high-quality candidates, screening applicants through meaningful assessments.
Cohort structure	The program is structured to provide mentorship and support for candidates.
Program context	
Effective program leadership	Program leaders are able to coordinate all stakeholders, obtain all necessary resources, and put critical program features into effect.
University-district partnerships	The program works with partners in substantive and operative ways that contribute to program sustainability.
Financial support	Program participants are given the support they need to complete the program.
State context	The program's standards are aligned with state standards, such as those related to program accreditation and school leader certification.

SOURCE: Evidence reviewed and compiled in Darling-Hammond et al. (2007).

NOTE: Darling-Hammond et al. (2007) identified a fifth program feature that is not part of the UPPI effort: continuous engagement with program participants, wherein the program offers induction coaching and support to graduates after they have been placed as principals.

In response to concerns about the state of initial principal preparation, The Wallace Foundation established the University Principal Preparation Initiative (UPPI). This four-year, $48.5 million initiative works toward redesigning universities' principal preparation programs with the support of high-need districts and according to the features and contexts recommended in the emerging evidence base on high-quality principal preparation (Table S.1). These features and contexts inform UPPI's three goals:

- Develop and implement high-quality courses of study and supportive organization conditions at universities where future principals receive their pre-service training.
- Foster strong collaborations between each university and its partner school districts.

- Develop state policies about program accreditation and principal licensure to promote higher-quality training statewide.

As of fall 2018, UPPI supports seven universities and their district or consortium partners. These are listed in Table S.2. Each partnership also includes a state partner and a mentor program.

Table S.2
UPPI Universities and District/Consortium Partners

University	District/Consortium Partners
Albany State University (ASU)	• Calhoun County Schools • Dougherty County School System • Pelham City Schools
Florida Atlantic University (FAU)	• Broward County Public Schools • School District of Palm Beach County • St. Lucie County Public Schools
North Carolina State University (NC State)	• Johnston County School District • Northeast Leadership Academy Consortium • Wake County Public School System
San Diego State University (SDSU)	• Chula Vista Elementary School District • San Diego Unified School District • Sweetwater Union High School District
University of Connecticut (UCONN)	• Hartford Public Schools • Meriden Public Schools • New Haven Public Schools
Virginia State University (VSU)	• Henrico County Public Schools • Hopewell City Public Schools • Sussex County Public Schools

Western Kentucky University (WKU)	• Green River Regional Educational Cooperative, represented initially by three member districts:
	  – Bowling Green Independent School District
	  – Owensboro Public Schools
	  – Simpson County Schools

To better understand the potential and challenges for this type of reform, The Wallace Foundation asked RAND Corporation researchers to conduct a five-year study of how UPPI programs are being implemented and the program's early results. The first part of the study, documented in the full version of this report, focuses on the implementation of UPPI in its first year, from fall 2016 to fall 2017, and addresses four research questions:

1. **Program Changes:** To what extent and in what ways have university programs modified their principal preparation programs?

2. **Management of the Redesign Process:** How did the university-based leads (ULs)—the individuals from each university leading the overall initiative at that site—manage the redesign process?

3. **Partner Engagement:** To what extent and how did partners (districts, state accrediting agency, mentor programs) support the program change?

4. **Challenges and Mitigating Strategies:** What challenges were encountered in the program redesign process, and how were they mitigated?

To answer these questions, we gathered data through site visits to the seven UPPI universities. We conducted interviews with the UL, university administrators, and leaders of the program, districts, state agency, and mentor program at each site. We also conducted focus groups with principal candidates, program faculty, and district principal mentors; observed UPPI team meetings; and reviewed literature, policy, and UPPI documents to gain insight into principal preparation program changes. The four research questions guided our data coding and analysis. Subsequent reports will offer in-depth assessments and analyses of state reform efforts, program implementation, and candidates' experiences in the redesigned program.

Findings Related to UPPI Implementation

The following findings address the early implementation of UPPI with respect to program changes, management of the redesign process, partner engagement, and challenges. These topics are ultimately interconnected.

Finding 1: UPPI programs began with some evidence-based features and contexts already in place.

Analysis of the data shows that many of the UPPI programs already had a number of the evidence-based features and contexts, summarized in Table S.1, in place before beginning the redesign process. For example, university programs had begun to build a **coherent curriculum** that prepared candidates for the demanding work of school principals, and to increase the use of instructors with administrative experience. Moreover, most of the selected programs began UPPI with a **clinical experience component** already in place, although some of these experiences did not reflect desired intensive learning experiences. For example, some programs required part-time internships with activities somewhat divorced from the real work of principals, whereas others required more sustained, on-the-job experiences. Several programs were already conducting **active recruiting**—that is, they had rigorous requirements and used performance-based tasks for candidate selection; other programs were using more traditional and test-based criteria. Most of the UPPI programs were already operating at least one district-based **cohort**; they had admitted a group of principal candidates from a given district and may have tailored curriculum and clinical experiences to the district needs. Those that did operate district-based cohorts indicated a desire to deepen or expand the cohort approach. Finally, the **districts** were committed to the effort—some of the districts had prior experiences working with the university programs, and **state policy** was generally consistent with the direction of the reform.

Finding 2: UPPI partnerships used the first year to develop a vision for the new program and the redesign process.

The process of "re-envisioning" the program provided an opportunity to examine and define guiding aspirations for the program, assess where development was needed, and begin to foster partnerships necessary for carrying out the work. The UPPI leadership teams engaged in three primary re-envisioning activities:

- **Standards development:** Each UPPI leadership team worked to develop or identify leader standards for the program. Program leader standards are broad performance expectations and goals for principal candidates graduating from each program. The process of developing standards brought teams together and contributed to identification of gaps in both the program leader standards and state and national leader standards.
- **Program assessment:** Each UPPI leadership team conducted an assessment to better understand the strengths and needs of its existing program. The teams used Quality Measures (QM; Education Development Center, 2009, 2018), a formative program assessment, to support such reflection. Most university programs and their partners described the QM exercise as a foundational experience that helped partners learn about one another's organizations and perspectives and that facilitated relationship-building. Although the insights generated through QM were not specific enough to support targeted program improvement, partners reported that QM helped their teams to identify gaps and areas of strength.
- **Logic model development:** Each UPPI leadership team worked to develop a logic model that would help guide change. Building logic models supported team-building by helping all partners understand the entire initiative and how the pieces worked together. Furthermore, in developing the logic model, the partners had an opportunity to share their thinking and be heard. This resulted in both a commitment to engage in the work and a logic model that reflected the perspectives of the stakeholders. Logic models took on many different forms but generally had four features, as illustrated in Figure S.1.

Finding 3: Each UPPI leadership team focused on redesigning its curriculum and instruction.

Curriculum changes aimed to create more coherent programs by (1) building on core ideas across courses, (2) developing cross-course assessments and assignments, and

Figure S.1
Common Features of a UPPI Redesign Logic Model

RESOURCES Organizations and materials	ACTIVITIES Key redesign tasks and strategies	OUTPUTS The redesigned program	OUTCOMES Intended impact
• UPPI project team • Partner organizations • Other state and national groups • Nonprofit organizations • Technical assistance providers • Leader standards	• Design curriculum and instruction • Develop clinical experiences • Establish more rigorous recruitment and selection processes • Coordinate activities around the leader tracking system	• UPPI program materials • Effective staff • Aligned curriculum • A leader tracking system	Some participants emphasized the development of transformational leaders or aimed for a model principal preparation program; others provided outcomes relevant to each partner (e.g., improved credentialing program or hiring practices)

(3) developing a tighter alignment between courses and clinical experiences. Moreover, in the redesigned curriculum, teams aimed to incorporate districts' perspectives and needs, as well as fill gaps identified through program re-envisioning activities. Some partnerships emphasized the application of adult education theory and research in redesigning their instructional approaches. These teams recognized that their adult students had potentially different learning needs than undergraduate and younger learners. For example, adult learners often bring prior work-related experiences to the classroom, and thus may be more able to engage in reflection based on experience. Teams also discussed greater use of interactive instructional strategies and the need to balance theory and practice.

Finding 4: UPPI leadership teams explored changes to clinical experiences and candidate recruitment and selection.

Although it is early in the process of redesigning clinical experiences, participating partnerships explored several changes in accordance with best practices and UPPI goals:

- aligning clinical experiences with standards and curricula
- providing candidates with realistic principal experiences
- extending the length of the clinical experience
- enhancing the mentoring, supervision, and evaluation of the candidates throughout the clinical experience.

Nearly all partnerships explicitly recognized that to develop practical knowledge and skills, candidates need structured opportunities to engage in activities that reflect the duties of a principal—which generally entails full-time, extended internships. Therefore, teams began to explore options for extending the clinical experience to better develop principal candidates. They also considered ways to improve mentoring, supervision, and evaluation in the clinical experience. For example, they explored limiting the mentor principal role to highly effective principals, training mentor principals, and shifting the university-based supervisor role so it is less about monitoring candidates for compliance with clinical experience expectations and more focused on actively coaching candidates and supporting their development.

Program redesign efforts also motivated all participating university programs to reflect on their recruitment and selection processes and work toward making them more in line with best practices. Most partnerships recognized a need to maintain or enhance the diversity of the candidate pool along various demographic dimensions, including gender, race, and ethnicity, and limiting selection to program candidates who aspire to be school leaders (i.e., not accepting all candidates willing to pay tuition) and who have the skills, abilities, and experiences needed to succeed in the program. Some teams considered how to effectively incorporate district input and in-depth, performance-based assessments into the candidate selection process.

Finding 5: University-based leads and actively engaged partners drove the initiative in the first year.

ULs in each program played a critical role in the redesign. The dedication, enthusiasm, management, and team-building skills of these leaders kept the initiative on track. It also was important that all organizations engaged on both a strategic and an operational level; staffing on the UPPI teams grew over the year to ensure capacity for this level of engagement. There was a strong emphasis on building and nurturing relationships among partners. Most partners recognized that openness, trust, and a culture of collaboration within teams were essential when working toward change. In part, this was accomplished by establishing a common vision and working backward from this vision to develop roles, responsibilities, and processes to reach partnership goals. Partners actively engaged in curriculum development either as part of cross-organization working groups or by reviewing key materials in their steering groups.

Finding 6: UPPI prompted partner states and districts to consider issues and/or undertake activities they may not have otherwise.

Engaging in the program redesign process prompted some states to consider—and even carry out—policy and practice changes, such as revising state-level leader standards, including the topic of leadership in state events, and scaling deep, formative program self-assessments. State partners also engaged with the UPPI leadership team to help carry out the redesign work, especially in providing guidance on how to align that work with state requirements. However, staff time limitations, as well as political sensitivities, limited state engagement in some cases.

Like states, through their participation in the redesign work, some districts have begun to reassess policies, such as those affecting district hiring practices. Some districts have also developed new collaborations with the university or with other districts. For example, one university-district partnership has begun to collaborate on an initiative to improve the diversity of the teaching workforce. Partly by design, the preparation program work at another site has begun to extend into professional development for sitting principals. Moreover, districts have begun to plan and build a leader tracking system (LTS), a required component of the UPPI effort. There is, however, some disconnect between the districts' expectations for such a data system (e.g., systematically collecting data on aspiring and sitting principals to guide development and placement decisions) and university programs' expectations (e.g., collecting data on program graduates to inform program improvements).

Finding 7: UPPI leadership teams developed strategies to mitigate the most pressing challenges, such as turnover and capacity limitations.

A range of institutional, or contextual, challenges threatened UPPI implementation. The most commonly reported challenge was turnover in leadership roles in UPPI teams or in a partner organization, which caused delays and threatened the continuity of support and vision for program redesign. Another type of contextual challenge involved institutional guidelines, such as lengthy hiring and course approval processes. Partnerships relied on ULs to mitigate these challenges and move the work forward. ULs did so by keeping the team focused on the goal, helping new leaders transition into the UPPI leadership team, and communicating with the university dean and provost about course approval and with state officials about implications of UPPI for policy. Some teams employed more-preemptive strategies (e.g., cross-training members for multiple roles in the UPPI leadership team and mapping deadlines for course approval) early on to help guard against contingencies.

Conclusions and Lessons Learned from the First Year of UPPI

The UPPI redesign process is complex. It involves multiple partners investing substantial time and effort into aligning priorities and long-range planning. Each of the seven UPPI leadership teams dedicated the first year to developing relationships, engaging partners, envisioning its redesigned principal preparation program, and beginning to redesign the program's curriculum. By all accounts, UPPI partner engagement was successful and sustained despite potential institutional barriers. Such engagement supported progress in curriculum redesign and planning of the LTS. In line with the goal of UPPI, advancements in program redesign moved toward evidence-based features. Smooth management of the redesign process depended on a shared vision, the drive of the UL, the establishment of work structures, and the application of tools and processes to support ongoing communication and collaboration.

UPPI partners identified several lessons learned from their first-year experiences. These can inform future UPPI-related principal preparation program reforms and other reforms conducted outside the UPPI effort:

- **Select partner organizations and individuals intentionally.** University respondents learned that, from the outset, selecting the right organizations to partner with and the right individuals within each organization to serve in key roles was crucial. University administrators defined desirable partner organizations as those that value innovative approaches to preparing leaders. Similarly, district partners expressed the importance of faculty being nimble and open to change. Ideally, all individuals working within a partnership should possess excellent communication skills, be a strong voice within their organization, be willing to advocate for UPPI-related activities and decisions, understand how to operationalize redesign ideas, and be able to see the big picture of the initiative.
- **Develop strong relationships early on to encourage commitment and progress.** Individuals from all seven UPPI programs reported learning the importance of developing strong relationships with district and state partners—both organizationally and individually—early in the initiative. Doing so helped to build commitment to both the redesign process and the redesigned program and helped ensure that each element of the program redesign would work to fulfill UPPI aims and meet the needs of each partner—despite inevitable obstacles.
- **It takes time and patience to achieve change.** Effecting change requires patience and commitment to a process that may seem painfully slow at times. While some ULs, leads from partner organizations, and others expressed frustration at the apparent slow pace of progress, they also recognized the benefit of taking the time, especially early on, to build a common understanding of goals, processes, and roles.

UPPI entails a systemic effort on the part of a network of at least four types of organizations (university, school districts or consortium, state agency, and mentor program), each with unique institutional and contextual backgrounds. It requires the partnerships to redesign four program features (curriculum and instruction, clinical experience, candidate recruitment and selection, and cohort structure), drawing on evidence on effective principal preparation, and to develop a leader tracking system to help inform continuous program improvement. Thus far, all seven partnerships appear to be standing up to the challenge: They have established a firm foundation of partnerships, articulated a common vision, developed approaches to manage the work, and initiated redesign of multiple program components.

Acknowledgments

We are grateful to the university-based leads at each of the seven universities participating in The Wallace Foundation's University Principal Preparation Initiative (UPPI) for spending many hours in interviews with us and facilitating interactions with their UPPI leadership teams. We also thank all the representatives of the partner organizations—districts, state departments of education, other state agencies, and mentor programs—who took the time to offer their perspectives on the program redesign process in hopes of helping other organizations learn from their experiences. In addition, we acknowledge the important insights into the initiative we received from many other individuals, including the provosts and deans from the universities, research and adjunct faculty members, supervising or mentor principals, and candidates in the principal preparation programs under redesign. Finally, we thank the project managers and coordinators who were instrumental in helping to plan our site visits, schedule data collection activities, and ensure that all visits went smoothly. This study would not have been possible without the input of all these individuals.

We would like to thank our contacts at The Wallace Foundation who provided critical and timely input about the design of this study through to the production of the full report. In particular, we have benefited significantly from feedback from Elizabeth Ty Wilde, Jody Spiro, Edward Pauly, Aiesha Eleusizov, Lucas Bernays Held, Rochelle Herring, Nicholas Pelzer, Andrew Cole, Jessica Schwartz, and Will Miller.

Our advisory group members were instrumental in helping us refine our study design and pushing us to think about the policy implications of this study. The members are Elaine Allensworth, Doug Anthony, Barnett Barry, Ann Clark, Brian Gill, Ellen Goldring, Erika Hunt, and Paul Manna. Also, our external reviewers, Christopher Nelson of RAND and Maryann Gray of the University of California, Los Angeles, provided valuable comments and guidance that helped us refine both the substance and the organization of our report.

Lastly, several RAND staff members supported the publishing of this report. Cathy Stasz provided insightful feedback on drafts of the report during the quality assurance process, and Kate Giglio, Paul Steinberg, James Torr, Donna White, and Lea Xenakis assisted with revisions and editing. The authors take full responsibility for any errors in the report.

Abbreviations

ASU	Albany State University
Ed.S.	education specialist
ESSA	Every Student Succeeds Act
FAU	Florida Atlantic University
FRPL	free- or reduced-price lunch
GPA	grade point average
K–12	kindergarten through 12th grade
LTS	leader tracking system
M.Ed.	master of education
M.S.	master of science
NC State	North Carolina State University
NELP	National Educational Leadership Preparation Standards
P–12	preschool through 12th grade
PSEL	Professional Standards for Educational Leaders
RFP	request for proposal
QM	Quality Measures
SDSU	San Diego State University
UCONN	University of Connecticut
UL	university-based lead (of UPPI)
UPPI	University Principal Preparation Initiative
VSU	Virginia State University
WKU	Western Kentucky University

CHAPTER ONE

Introduction

School leaders play a pivotal role in school improvement (Grissom and Loeb, 2011; Harvey and Holland, 2013; Knapp et al., 2010; Louis et al., 2010). As we learn more about the importance of school leaders and the complexity of their jobs, school districts, policymakers, and the public are making increasing demands for highly competent leaders. At the turn of the millennium, many public school districts in the United States faced a crisis in school leadership. This crisis was characterized by several challenges: high turnover, difficulties in finding replacements for departing principals, and a perception that newly hired principals lacked the skills to succeed in their positions (Gates, Ringel, and Santibanez, 2003). In addition, traditional university-based principal preparation programs, the largest producer of new principals in the nation, were found to be inadequate in preparing graduates for the challenges of principalship in today's schools (Bottoms and O'Neill, 2001; Briggs et al., 2013; Manna, 2015).

In response, The Wallace Foundation commissioned a synthesis of four reports that highlighted the shortcomings in university principal preparation programs (Davis, 2016).[1] The findings were significant. The synthesis found that both university programs producing school leaders and school districts hiring the graduates of these programs were dissatisfied with the quality of the preparation programs. For example, many universities believed their principal preparation programs needed improvement. More than one-third of the representatives from colleges and universities that were surveyed by American Association of Colleges for Teacher Education—which represents most college- or university-based principal preparation programs—reported that their existing programs prepared graduates "not well" or only "somewhat well." Moreover, leaders of school districts that employ program graduates were largely dissatisfied with

---

[1] One of the four reports documents the University Council for Educational Administration's (UCEA's) survey of its 97 members about their interest in and eligibility to participate in a university principal preparation program redesign initiative. Fifty-nine members responded. UCEA's members may be considered more predisposed to change. For the second report, the American Association of Colleges for Teacher Education received 255 survey responses from its 842 member universities, which represent more conventional principal preparation programs. The third report, completed by American Institutes for Research, reviewed laws and regulations of the states. The final report, by the American Association of School Administrators, was based on survey responses from more than 400 superintendents across 42 states.

the quality of the programs. Among the superintendents surveyed, 80 percent felt that program improvements were necessary. On average, the superintendents rated the level of preparation as less than effective on each one of a set of 15 common school leader responsibilities that programs ought to prepare candidates for, including recruiting and selecting teachers, making decisions, problem-solving, and using data.

These findings provided a catalyst for redesigning principal training programs. Following the 2016 investigations, The Wallace Foundation next sought to help university principal training programs meet ongoing challenges through its University Principal Preparation Initiative (UPPI). This four-year, $48.5 million initiative began in July 2016 and now supports seven universities, their district and state partners, and mentor programs. UPPI works toward redesigning the universities' principal preparation programs in high-need districts according to evidence-based principles and practices, which may, in turn, model, inspire, and mobilize other principal preparation programs toward transformation. In particular, UPPI was designed to achieve three goals:

- Develop and implement high-quality courses of study and supportive organization conditions at universities where future principals receive their pre-service training.
- Foster strong collaborations between each university and its partner school districts.
- Develop state policies about program accreditation and principal licensure to promote higher-quality training statewide.

The Wallace Foundation asked RAND Corporation researchers to conduct a five-year study to assist in understanding how UPPI programs are being implemented and the impact UPPI programs are having in areas of desired change, including state policies. This report provides an assessment of the first year of UPPI implementation, focusing specifically on university program changes, the management of the program redesign process, partner engagement, and challenges and strategies to address them. This report is the first in a series of ongoing work. Subsequent reports will offer in-depth assessments and analyses of state reform efforts, program implementation, and candidates' experiences in the redesigned program.

Background: Evidence Supports the Need for and Goals of UPPI

UPPI was developed to inform changes necessary for today's principal preparation programs. The need for the initiative, as well as its goals, are grounded in evidence. We summarize related research in this section to provide background on the need for UPPI, the development of UPPI goals, and our findings.

In 2007, Darling-Hammond et al. conducted groundbreaking research in which the research team identified features of effective principal preparation programs and the context in which such programs operate. In the ensuing decade, the importance of these program features and context elements were affirmed and extended by experts in the field. The research indicated that high-quality principal preparation programs are coherent,[2] evidence-based, and aligned with required state or voluntary professional standards, and that they use data for continuous quality improvement. Such programs have the following features:

- **A coherent curriculum** (one in which the content aligns and builds across courses) focused on instruction and school improvement that integrates theory and practice through active learning and input from faculty with experience in school administration
- **Supervised clinical experiences** linked to coursework, with opportunities for program participants to engage in realistic leadership activities over a long period of time and obtain constructive feedback from effective principals
- **Active recruiting** of high-quality applicants and screening applicants using authentic assessments that reflect the real work for principals
- **Cohort structure** to mentor and support candidates in their professional learning
- **Continuous engagement with program participants** after they have been placed as principals by providing induction coaching and support (Darling-Hammond et al., 2007, p. 145; Larsen et al., 2016a, 2016b).

The research also found that effective programs operate in supportive contexts marked by the following:

- **Effective program leadership.** Darling-Hammond et al. (2007) suggest that "[l]eaders who had the vision, commitment, and capacity to coordinate stakeholders, secure resources and implement the critical features well" are necessary (p. 147).
- **Partnerships between university programs and districts.** Darling-Hammond et al. (2007) found that exemplary programs used such partnerships in a variety of ways to address a range of substantive and operational issues and to contribute to sustainability. What the programs had in common was a willingness on the part of key actors in the districts and the university to collaborate as needed.
- **Financial support.** Program participants may need assistance from the university, district, state, or private organizations.

---

2   The term *coherent* is used to describe various aspects of exemplary programs. Although a specific definition is not offered, we infer, based on standard dictionary definitions of the term, that it is being used to describe programs that are cohesive, coordinated, clear, and logically ordered or integrated.

- **A state context that uses required standards.** State organizations can help drive program improvement through accreditation and school leader certification guidelines. They can also help provide support for current and aspiring administrators.

What Is Lacking in University-Based Principal Preparation Programs?

To date, little is known about the prevalence of such program and contextual features in today's university-based principal preparation programs. The limited amount we do know comes from analyses of curricula, surveys of practicing principals and district officials, and examinations of existing programs. Together, this work suggests that although some programs have incorporated some of these features, such features are not prevalent. As noted earlier, many district leaders feel that existing programs do not prepare their future principals sufficiently (Davis, 2016). Principals have also noted insufficient preparation: Davis reports that, in a national survey of school principals, about half of the respondents rated programs as poor to fair in preparing them to deal with diverse school environments and in-school policies. In another study, 89 percent of surveyed principals said that the schools of education they attended did not prepare graduates to cope with classroom realities (Levine, 2005).

Existing analyses of university-based principal preparation programs show that a number of key features that make such programs successful are lacking:

Coherent curriculum. The curricula in principal preparation programs do not emphasize leadership skills that have a demonstrated relationship with school and student success and that are most relevant to the work of today's principals. Instead, most programs emphasize technical content. A systematic review of a stratified national sample of curricula from school leader preparation programs found that most programs spend an average of 30 percent of course time on technical knowledge, such as law, finance, and research skills, and only 11 percent of time on instructional leadership (Hess and Kelly, 2007). Similarly, less than 5 percent of course weeks are spent learning how to use data or to manage school improvement. Only 2 percent of course weeks are spent learning how to connect school management with accountability.

Supervised clinical experiences. Research suggests that effective principal preparation involves clinical experiences that are linked to coursework to provide realistic opportunities for candidates to learn the critical competencies required of principals. Although 94 percent of surveyed colleges with educator preparation programs report that their institutions have strong clinical experiences (Davis, 2016), a survey of 61 principal preparation programs found that only about one-third reported providing internships that build a comprehensive understanding of principals' work (Fry, Bottoms, and O'Neill, 2005). There is also evidence that internships do not emphasize the most important skills principals need to learn: Surveyed candidates reported spending most of their time in clinical experiences on testing and discipline (Sherman and Cunningham, 2006). Further, programs struggle to provide effective supervision: More than a third of principal preparation programs reported that they do not believe they have or could offer high-quality mentoring in the clinical experiences (Davis, 2016).

The limitations of the clinical experience may be an artifact of the time allocated. Ninety-three percent of school leadership programs surveyed reported that the major-ity of their students attended part-time (Wilmore and Bratlien, 2005). Most candi-dates continued to teach full time while enrolled in the principal preparation program; almost half of programs surveyed indicated that lack of funding for clinical experiences could affect quality (Davis, 2016). In terms of clinical experiences, this means that candidates must seize small pockets of time to complete discrete administrative tasks rather than experience the full principal role (Levine, 2005). Demanding intensive clinical experiences is not a state priority: Only 14 states require that candidates spend at least 300 hours in field-based experiences (Davis, 2016).

Selective admissions criteria and process. Whereas strong principal prepara-tion programs emphasize the recruitment and selection of high-quality candidates who are committed to becoming principals, university principal preparation programs have a history of low admission standards and a reputation for easy degrees (Levine, 2005). Because many states and school districts offer financial incentives for teachers to obtain (any) graduate degree, some universities have developed principal preparation programs with broad appeal to candidates beyond those with an explicit interest in becoming a principal. Relaxed admission standards can boost enrollment and increase revenue for the university, but they pose challenges for the development of rigorous professional programs—particularly if the satisfaction of a majority of participants is unrelated to success in preparing candidates for the principalship (Levine, 2005).

Strong university-district partnerships. Strong partnerships between univer-sities and school districts are another hallmark of effective programs, but a national survey of district superintendents suggests that such partnerships are infrequent. Eighty-nine percent of superintendents surveyed reported that university-district col-laboration happened only sometimes or never, and 22 percent did not feel that existing principal preparation programs had strong partnerships (Davis, 2016). Again, state policies have not encouraged such relationships; fewer than half of states have policies about developing district-program partnerships (Davis, 2016).

Why University-Based Principal Preparation Programs May Not Make the Grade

Principal preparation programs have been slow to adopt the evidence-based features of effective programs, and some studies suggest that a range of barriers hinder imple-mentation, although such barriers have not been empirically validated. They include the following:

- **University officials may not support change.** Program directors reported "poor university administration and support" and that university officials showed "a lack of real commitment to the program" and "a lack of urgency for change" (Davis, 2016, p. 13).

- **Faculty within the program may not see a need to change.** Tenure-track professors are rewarded for research publications rather than clinical work, so university reward systems would need to change to motivate professors.
- **It can be difficult to hire and motivate the best instructors.** The requirement of a doctorate to teach in a university program can prevent otherwise qualified practitioners from teaching. Low faculty salaries also undermine efforts to hire the best instructors.
- **Lack of funds constrain quality programming.** Insufficient financial support limits salaries and clinical experiences, as well as program offerings.
- **State principal licensure and program accreditation policies limit program change.** Complex policies that are difficult to navigate slow the pace or limit the nature of program change (Davis, 2016; Hale and Moorman, 2003).

Previous Reform Efforts

Prior efforts to redesign teacher and principal preparation programs can provide some context for the current effort. The Holmes Group, with its 90 constituent universities, aimed to accomplish many of the same goals as UPPI for teacher preparation in the mid 1980s: develop partnerships between kindergarten through 12th grade (K–12) schools and teacher preparation programs, include practitioners as program faculty, and improve the content and rigor of the preparation programs (Holmes Group, 1990; 1995; Stallings, Wiseman, and Knight, 1995). Teachers for a New Era also aimed to improve collaboration between K–12 schools and universities, with teachers serving as faculty. Under this initiative, participating universities—and their district partners—received grants from the Carnegie Foundation, engaged university leadership, and participated in professional learning communities with their fellow grantees (McDiarmid and Caprino, 2017).

Both of these earlier teacher preparation program redesign efforts identified role parity as a priority, aiming for schools to be full partners in the initiative. UPPI's design involves district-level leadership, which may help promote role parity, in part because the district leaders identified for UPPI have greater decisionmaking authority than school leaders and in part because schools are constrained as players by district policy. Many of the other features used by prior teacher preparation program redesign efforts, such as creating learning communities for the partnerships, are also integrated in UPPI.

More recently, there have been efforts to offer innovative principal preparation programs (Hudson, 2016; Phillips, 2013). For example, the University of Illinois at Chicago created a program for aspiring principals with rigorous admission criteria and clinical experiences. In addition, The Wallace Foundation has been supporting six school districts to, among other goals, partner with principal preparation programs to improve the principal preparation pipeline. The question remains whether and how universities—by far the biggest producers of new principals—can evolve their principal preparation programs to meet the urgent need for quality school leaders by aligning with the current knowledge base of research and best practices.

Overview: University Principal Preparation Initiative

UPPI seeks to address the question: "How can university principal preparation programs—working in partnership with high-need school districts, mentor preparation programs, and the state—improve their training so it reflects the evidence on how best to prepare effective principals?" The initiative emphasizes many of the effective program features identified by prior research in the previous section. These include a comprehensive curriculum (a course of study, including content and organization of courses, that integrates theory and practice); well-supervised, extended internships with opportunities to experience the real work of principals; higher standards for recruitment and performance-based assessments to guide selection; and a cohort structure. In addition to the evidence-based program features, UPPI also calls for teams to develop conditions that are likely to support successful redesign by building strong university-district partnerships and exploring ways in which state policy could better support strong principal preparation.

University programs identified their district and state partners when applying for the grant. They collaborated with those partners on a grant proposal, which required evidence of commitment from all partners. The university-district partnerships are at the core of the UPPI work. Since program participants will ultimately be seeking jobs in school districts, districts provide a critical perspective on the context, needs, and challenges of real schools and the qualifications needed for successful school leaders. Programs may be designed to draw on these district perspectives to shape the curriculum and instruction in the program and improve the fit of the graduates to districts and schools. Districts can help design and provide rich field experiences and sustained internships where candidates can apply their classroom learning and receive on-the-job mentorship. Districts can also advise on and support the recruitment and selection of principal candidates to help ensure that qualified and promising candidates who intend to take on a principalship and grow in that role are guided into the preparation program. Finally, districts are positioned to track and provide feedback to university programs on their graduates' placements and performance—feedback that may lead to continuous program revisions and improvement.

These university-district partnerships work in a large policy environment that is dominated by state-level policies. Because state policies on program accreditation, principal licensure, and leader standards may support or suppress redesign efforts, UPPI is designed to deliberately engage state partners in the work—a feature that has not been emphasized in most other principal preparation reforms. By including a state partner, UPPI aspires to stimulate state-level policy changes that support the systemic improvement of principal preparation programs within the state.

The UPPI partners made a commitment to carry out the core required elements of UPPI: redesign the program curriculum and instruction, the clinical experiences, and the recruitment and selection processes, and develop leader tracking systems (LTSs) to inform continuous improvements of the programs. State partners further committed to reviewing their policies that affect university-based principal preparation and work with stakeholders to consider and potentially enact policy changes. Specifically, the goals for the first year were to begin the curriculum redesign, begin designing the LTS, and bring together stakeholders to discuss how the state can support high-quality principal preparation. Most of the curriculum design work was expected to occur during the first two years of the initiative.

The Wallace Foundation offered a range of supports to universities and their district and state partners for their redesign efforts. First, universities and their partners selected a mentor program—a traditional or alternative principal preparation program that has particular expertise in one or more areas that the UPPI university program is seeking to develop. Second, The Wallace Foundation hosts professional learning communities among the sites and, separately, for university-based leads (ULs; the individual from each university leading the overall initiative at that site), program faculty, and state department representatives. Professional learning communities are groups composed of professionals that meet regularly to share their experiences and expertise and to collaborate on efforts to improve their professional craft (DuFour, 2004). At these multiday meetings, all UPPI teams were invited to learn from other teams engaging in the same redesign work. Third, partnerships have access to technical assistance providers to help with program self-assessments, LTS design, and standards alignment.

The UPPI design provides partnerships with a fair amount of flexibility to develop their own vision and approach within the broad areas of redesign (e.g., curriculum, clinical experiences). This flexibility fits the state of the research and the nature of the UPPI endeavor. Although we know something about effective principal preparation program practices, we know very little about effective ways to transform traditional preparation programs. Therefore, each partnership is tasked with finding the path for transformation that works for its context, with the hope that the programs will both succeed themselves and serve as models for others.

Programs and UPPI Partnerships Overview

Through an application process, The Wallace Foundation selected a university principal preparation program in each of seven states to participate in UPPI. These programs were selected in part because they had expressed interest and conducted some initial work toward redesign and were located in states that had or were exploring policies or practices favorable to improving principal training:

- Albany State University in Albany, Georgia
- Florida Atlantic University in Boca Raton, Florida
- North Carolina State University in Raleigh, North Carolina
- San Diego State University in San Diego, California
- University of Connecticut in Storrs, Connecticut
- Virginia State University in Petersburg, Virginia
- Western Kentucky University in Bowling Green, Kentucky.

These seven universities are all public institutions, but they vary on other features. While some are in major cities, others are in more rural regions. Three are minority-serving institutions, and two are land-grant universities. Two universities offer programs aimed at developing turnaround principals. Moreover, the seven universities include Research 1, Research 2, Master's 1, and Master's 2 institutions.[3] Appendix A contains a detailed description of each program at baseline and of each organization involved in a UPPI partnership. Highlights are presented in Table 1.1.

Five of the seven universities partnered with three districts. One university worked with two districts and a consortium of smaller districts, and another university partnered with a large consortium initially represented by three member districts. The district/consortium partners were all high-need in some respect (e.g., serve a high proportion of minority students or students from low-income households, have low-performing schools, or are located in rural areas), which was a criterion for UPPI site selection. However, the district/consortium partners differed in size, urbanicity, and the demographics of the students they serve.

The diversity among universities and their district partners is of particular note. Many prior education studies have focused on large universities and large, urban school districts, partly because size matters in conducting quantitative research. As such, this set of UPPI universities and school districts provides a unique window into principal preparation in commonly occurring but rarely studied contexts.

Within each partner organization, a senior leader manages the UPPI effort. By design and de facto, senior engagement helps raise the organization's commitment to the initiative. Typically, the program director or department chair at the university leads the grant, in close collaboration with associate superintendents from the school districts and senior staff from the state organizations and mentor programs. This group, accompanied by a varying cast of characters from the partner organizations, forms the

---

[3] According to the Carnegie Classification System (Carnegie Foundation, 2017), colleges and universities are identified against specific criteria as *Research* (grant at least 20 doctoral degrees), *Master's* (grant at least 50 master's and fewer than 20 doctoral degrees), *Baccalaureate* (at least 50 percent baccalaureate or higher, fewer than 50 master's or 20 doctoral degrees), and *Baccalaureate/Associate's*. Research schools are further sorted into *R1* (highest research activity), *R2* (higher research activity), and *R3* (moderate research activity). Master's schools are further sorted into *M1* (larger), *M2* (medium), and *M3* (smaller).

Table 1.1
UPPI Universities and Partners

University	District/Consortium Partners	State Partner	Mentor Program(s)
Albany State University (ASU)	• Calhoun County Schools • Dougherty County School System • Pelham City Schools	• Georgia Professional Standards Commission	• Quality-Plus Leader Academy (QPLA) • New York City Leadership Academy (NYCLA)
Florida Atlantic University (FAU)	• Broward County Public Schools • School District of Palm Beach County • St. Lucie County Public Schools	• Florida Department of Education	• University of Denver
North Carolina State University (NC State)	• Johnston County School District • Northeast Leadership Academy Consortium • Wake County Public School System	• North Carolina Department of Public Instruction	• University of Denver
San Diego State University (SDSU)	• Chula Vista Elementary School District • San Diego Unified School District • Sweetwater Union High School District	• California Commission on Teacher Credentialing	• University of Washington
University of Connecticut (UCONN)	• Hartford Public Schools • Meriden Public Schools • New Haven Public Schools	• Connecticut State Department of Education	• University of Illinois at Chicago • New York City Leadership Academy
Virginia State University (VSU)	• Henrico County Public Schools • Hopewell City Public Schools • Sussex County Public Schools	• Virginia Department of Education	• Quality-Plus Leader Academy

Western Kentucky University (WKU)	• Green River Regional Educational Cooperative, represented initially by three member districts:
	  – Bowling Green Independent School District
	  – Owensboro Public Schools
	  – Simpson County Schools
		• Kentucky Education Professional Standards Board	• University of Illinois at Chicago

core team for the redesign effort. Most of the senior leaders were in place before UPPI began, but personnel and organizational structures have evolved.

National Policy Context in Which UPPI Is Situated

Around the launch of UPPI, two significant developments related to school leader development were playing out at the national level (see Appendix B for additional detail). First, in October 2015, a new set of national Professional Standards for Educational Leaders (PSEL; National Policy Board for Educational Administration, 2015) was approved. PSEL provides a research-based benchmark of what constitutes effective school leadership. As part of UPPI, teams were asked to evaluate how well their vision aligned with PSEL. Meanwhile, the complementary National Educational Leadership Preparation (NELP) standards (University Council for Educational Administration, 2018), the basis for principal preparation program accreditation, were available for use beginning January 2018. NELP standards deal specifically with program content but reflect some findings from Darling-Hammond et al.'s (2007) study overviewed above. Specifically, one standard promotes having students engage in "a substantial and sustained educational leadership internship experience."

Second, the Every Student Succeeds Act (ESSA; Pub. L. 114-95, 2015)—a reauthorization of the federal Elementary and Secondary Education Act (Pub. L. 89-10, 1965)—was signed into law in 2015. It signaled the importance of school leadership by providing opportunities for states to use federal funds to pursue initiatives—including principal preparation programs—that would improve the quality and effectiveness of principals and other school leaders (Herman et al., 2017). Thus, state-level leadership in UPPI states was simultaneously revisiting its state principal preparation policies as part of its role as UPPI partners and considering whether and how to improve its school leadership approaches under ESSA.

Scope of This Report and Overview of Study Methods

Our study examines the primary goals of UPPI and the resulting program changes by addressing following research questions:

1. **Program Changes:** To what extent and in what ways have university programs modified their principal preparation programs?
2. **Management of the Redesign Process:** How did the ULs manage the redesign process?
3. **Partner Engagement:** To what and how extent did partners (districts, state accrediting agency, mentor programs) support the program change?
4. **Challenges and Strategies:** What challenges were encountered in the program redesign process, and how were they addressed?
5. **Changes in Candidates' Experiences:** What changes in candidates' experiences can be observed and measured within the five-year study time frame?

The focus of this report is on the first four research questions. However, we do not answer these questions as if they were in silos. Management and partner engagement, for example, are closely intertwined, and challenges and solutions arise in relation to program change, management, and engagement. The report thus reflects a more holistic picture of initial implementation.

A central goal of this study is to generate lessons that other university principal preparation programs and their partners within the selected state and across the county can adopt or adapt as they undertake their own principal preparation system improvement efforts. In line with this, the initial implementation study seeks to identify themes that cut across sites. Even in doing so, we attempted to recognize and attend to the unique context of each university program and its specific approach to UPPI. For example, while we focus on cross-site themes throughout this report, we present selected examples that are grounded in specific programs for illustrative purposes.

We gathered data for this report throughout 2017. Two-person teams conducted site visits in spring 2017 to the seven universities and returned for a second site visit in fall 2017. Each site visit consisted of interviews with the UL heading the redesign and persons leading the effort from the program, districts, state agency, and mentor program. In the spring, we also interviewed university administrators and conducted focus groups with principal candidates, program faculty, and district mentors. Topics tracked efforts to answer the first four research questions.

When we visited the sites in fall 2017, we observed a scheduled UPPI leadership team meeting, during which the core team discussed issues, worked on a redesign task, or otherwise conducted business as usual. We also collected documents, such as program handbooks and syllabi, that characterized the university program and relevant district and state policies prior to UPPI. Finally, on a regular (e.g., monthly) basis after the initial site visit, we conducted brief phone or online check-ins with the UL and the lead of each partner district.

All interview and focus group data were transcribed, coded, and analyzed in Dedoose (SocioCultural Research Consultants, 2016), a cross-platform Internet application that assists with qualitative data. Data analysis was guided by analytical questions keyed to the first four primary research questions. For more information about data collection and analysis, see Appendix C.

Key Terms

Throughout the report, we use the term *partnership* or *team* to refer to each of the seven multi-organization partnerships (including university program, district partners, state partner, and mentor program) involved in UPPI. A *mentor program* supports the university in the redesign effort. A mentor program is a traditional or alternative principal preparation program that has particular expertise in one or more areas that the UPPI university program is seeking to develop. Within the initiative, it is sometimes known as the *partner provider program*.

We use the term *UPPI leadership team* to refer to the multi-organization team that leads UPPI activities at each site. The individual from each university leading the overall initiative at each site is the *university-based lead* (UL). At the minimum, each UPPI leadership team also includes at least one *lead* from each partner organization (i.e., district partner lead, state partner lead, mentor program lead). Leads head the effort for their organization and serve as liaisons between their and other organizations.

We use the term *university administrator* to refer to the dean, provost, or president. Students enrolled in a principal preparation program are principal *candidates*, whereas we refer to individuals applying to (but not yet selected or enrolled) in such a program as *applicants*. Finally, we use the term *mentor principal* to refer to active principals or district leaders who supervise and evaluate principal candidates' clinical experience, and the term *university-based supervisor* to denote the program staff members that oversee the candidates' clinical experience. We use the term *clinical experience* to include what may otherwise be called field experience, practical experience, or internship, although we recognize that there are nuanced differences among these.

Throughout the report, we use quantifiers to indicate the number of sites that engaged in a certain activity, expressed a certain idea, or discussed a certain theme. We use *few* or *some* to mean fewer than half (e.g., 1–3 of the sites); *most* means more than half (e.g., 4–6 of the sites); and *all* means all (e.g., 7 out of the 7 sites).

Organization of This Report

This report presents findings from the first (2016–2017) of four years of UPPI implementation. It is designed to provide preliminary insights on the first four research questions shown above. We describe the UPPI sites, emphasizing their starting points and efforts to launch their program redesign efforts. We start in Chapter Two by sharing the UPPI leadership teams' efforts to re-envision their program and launch the redesign. In Chapter Three, we report progress with respect to the redesign efforts. In Chapter Four, we explore the leadership and management of the redesign progress. In Chapter Five, we discuss how the context in which the principal preparation programs operate has changed. Each of these chapters touches on partner engagement as well as challenges encountered by the teams and strategies for addressing them.

The report also includes three appendixes. Appendix A contains a detailed description of each program at baseline and of each organization involved in a UPPI partnership. Appendix B provides more details on the two significant developments (mentioned above) related to school leadership development that were playing out at the national level when UPPI was being launched. Appendix C contains more information about our data collection and analysis approach for the study.

CHAPTER TWO

Re-Envisioning the Program

All seven university principal preparation programs began participating in UPPI with some of the desired program elements in place and a tentative plan for achieving the full redesign that they expected to revise and reshape. In fact, much of the work for the first year involved taking stock. The UPPI leadership teams began the redesign work by engaging in activities intended to ensure that their programs would be coherent, evidence-based, and aligned to state and national leader standards. These activities involved (1) coming to agreement with partners about the desired end point ("beginning with the end in mind"), (2) taking stock of the current program, and (3) developing a roadmap to get from the current point to the desired end point. The UPPI programs also reflected on the context in which their programs were operating and on ways in which that context needed to improve.

During the first year of the initiative, the UPPI leadership teams refined their goals for the redesign work by developing program leader standards, evaluated their current program using a formative assessment, Quality Measures (QM; Education Development Center, 2018), and outlined conceptually how they intended to achieve those goals by creating a redesign logic model. The Wallace Foundation provided structure and support for these efforts and established timelines for completion. This process of revisiting the goals and process of the redesign served two functions: (1) push the partners to consider and make fundamental changes when needed, and (2) build the partnerships necessary to carry out the redesign work.

In this chapter, we present and discuss key findings from the re-envisioning effort.

Principal Preparation Programs Reflected Some of the Evidence-Based Characteristics Prior to UPPI

Prior to joining UPPI, the seven principal preparation programs already reflected some of the characteristics of evidence-based programs. As summarized in Chapter One, the curricula of effective principal preparation programs tend to be coherent, focus on developing instructional and school improvement leadership, integrate theory and practice, provide opportunities for active learning, and use instructors who have experience as school administrators.

University programs had begun to incorporate real work experiences, or learning experiences that replicate real work, prior to UPPI but recognized the need to build a coherent curriculum that prepared candidates for the demands of the job. A coherent curriculum gives the candidate a unified experience, in which classes build on each other and fieldwork reinforces classroom instruction. Several of the programs had aligned their fieldwork and coursework prior to UPPI; however, most programs voiced a need to integrate their stand-alone courses into a coherent whole, moving away from "disparate courses that don't really speak to each other."

Several ULs reported that they were already integrating practice into their courses, using "authentic, integrated leadership exercises," inquiry learning, and performance-based assessments in their coursework. For example, one program required that at least 50 percent of courses include performance-based work for which the candidate must complete a task or resolve an issue, rather than respond to multiple-choice-style test questions. Part of integrating the practice perspective in the preparation program was to ensure that candidates are taught by instructors with firsthand knowledge of school administration. Most of the selected programs began UPPI with at least some instructors having prior or current administrative experience. Prior to UPPI, however, the extent or depth of the theory-practice integration was not clear.

Prior research suggests that effective programs focus on developing school improvement leadership. The selected programs began UPPI already committed to improving leadership for schools enrolling underserved populations. For example, one program emphasized school improvement leadership by providing incentives for candidates to focus on low-performing schools. Two universities highlighted the alignment of UPPI with their land-grant mission to focus on high-need, high-poverty areas across the state. Three universities are historically black colleges or universities or are Hispanic-serving; one UPPI leadership team indicated that being a minority-serving institution helped the university meet "the needs of the most challenged schools in the districts we serve."

Although there were notable exceptions, most of the selected programs began UPPI with clinical experience requirements that did not reflect the desired intensive learning experiences. Effective principal preparation programs tend to have extended internships that involve carrying out real principal tasks and getting constructive feedback from effective mentor principals. Initially, the clinical experiences of UPPI programs were mixed. Some programs required candidates to complete a selection of assignments at their own school in nonteaching hours while the candidates continued to teach full-time. Other programs offered more intense, sustained clinical experiences in which their principal candidates worked hands-on in the principal role. At the extreme, the clinical experience could be quite intense. For example, one program required a paid, yearlong, full-time clinical experience, supported through state fellowship stipends, for principal candidates training to serve high-need, rural schools. That was not typical for most programs at the beginning of UPPI.

Some universities had already instituted selective recruitment and a cohort structure in their programs. According to prior research, effective principal preparation programs actively recruit high-quality candidates and screen them using their performance on problem-solving tasks or simulations. Prior to UPPI, several UPPI sites already had a rigorous selection process and used performance-based tasks for selection into one or more of their preparation programs. However, other programs had traditional acceptance requirements, such as a master's degree and a grade point average of 3.0 or higher.

Most of the UPPI programs were already operating at least one district-based cohort, meaning that they admitted a group of principal candidates from a given district and that they may have tailored curriculum and clinical experiences to the district needs. Those that did operate with cohorts indicated a desire to deepen or expand the cohort approach.

Principal Preparation Programs Operated in a Favorable Context

The principal preparation programs selected for UPPI already had some of the features of evidence-based programs in place. They had relationships with districts that were receptive to the work and were located in states with a favorable context for program reform. UPPI provided them an opportunity to deepen existing partnerships and build new ones.

ULs reported intentionally selecting partner districts that had the capacity and interest to engage deeply. In addition to prioritizing high-need districts and taking into consideration district size and proximity, the universities sought partner districts with qualities they thought would foster collaboration. They considered, for example, districts whose interests aligned with the university program, that is, those that expressed a desire for more rigorous principal preparation programs and had strategic plans that aligned with the university's vision for principal preparation. In one selected district, for instance, three main pillars of the district strategic plan—talent development, recruitment and selection of high performers, and leadership pathways for employees—focused on identifying and developing stronger principals.

ULs also looked to districts they deemed trustworthy and committed, based on their prior interactions and relationships. Most universities selected at least one district with which they already had an established principal preparation pipeline. These districts already had a stake in the university program and working relationships with the university's program staff. Across all of the partnerships, eight districts had such a formal relationship with their university, characterized by an established, official principal preparation program with the university that entailed memorandums of understanding between the two entities. Some universities selected UPPI partner districts with which they did not have such formal partnership but with which they did have other ties. For example, the district leads served as adjunct professors in the program, or schools in the district regularly served as clinical experience sites for principal candidates. ULs reported thinking that leveraging prior relationships would help them launch the initiative efficiently and smoothly because inside knowledge about the partner organizations could help manage the redesign. Still, 11 partner districts from six of the seven sites had no prior relationship with the university program beyond hiring its graduates.

ULs sought visionary partners. The ULs also reported considering the characteristics of, and relationships with, individuals who led the districts as a factor in choosing partners. Most ULs reported strategically seeking individuals who were "forward thinking" and "visionary," and whom they trusted would commit to the UPPI work and deliver, regardless of competing priorities. ULs had learned from prior interactions that these district leads were effective at championing a cause they believed in, at mobilizing their staff to get work done, and at communicating openly about their perspectives. In addition, in cases where ULs and district leads have a prior professional relationship at an individual level, a degree of comfort with each other and channels of communication had already been established.

State partners supported program redesign. The states in which the programs were housed already had some supportive policies (e.g., state-level leader standards) in place and were actively exploring additional policies (e.g., using Every Student Succeeds Act funds to support school leader development) when UPPI began.

Identifying Program-Level Leader Standards Contributed to Shared Vision

An early UPPI requirement was to identify or develop program-level leader standards that would guide the redesign work. Such standards were meant to identify what a principal that graduates from the specific program should know and be able to do. The process of developing these standards represented an opportunity for partners—district partners in particular—to provide input about the type and characteristics of school leaders needed. The activity of identifying program-level leader standards involved the core UPPI leadership team and generally took place over several team meetings.

Program-level leader standards reflected a shared vision of effective principals. The program-level leader standards each team arrived at served as broad performance expectations and goals for principal candidates graduating from each program. In most cases, these leader standards also represented the major concepts and competencies that the curriculum and clinical experience of the programs intended to address. In all, the standards are what team members from the program and partner districts, and in some cases the state agency, all agreed were necessary skills and competencies for any principal to have, perhaps especially principals in the particular region the university program served.

Most of the UPPI leadership teams identified about 7–15 standards, organized under major domains of principal leadership (e.g., leadership in vision-setting and strategic thinking, instructional leadership, organizational management leadership). For some programs, each standard incorporated more fine-grained indicators. Standards that teams commonly identified related to leaders setting and communicating visions, supporting instruction and learning, developing teacher leaders, and establishing a positive school culture. Two teams had a standalone standard for family and community engagement: One team championed "leading with courage" (e.g., by addressing contextual challenges and encouraging risk-taking), and one team elevated equity-focused leadership and building relationships by wrapping these two principles around all other standards.

Some UPPI leadership teams developed new program-level leader standards, while others adapted or adopted state or national standards. Three partnerships created new program standards through bottom-up development processes, with development beginning essentially from scratch (versus starting by revising or revisiting current program standards or expectations and iterating from there). Such processes were organized around identifying a shared aspirational vision for future graduates of their program in collaboration with their district partners. For example, the core steering committee from one program spent a lot of time developing its values and beliefs, crosswalking them to program and professional standards, and drilling down to district-level standards ("Districts have their own DNA"). This team used those standards to backward-map to the program, asking, "What do our students need to be able to do to master all the standards?" One partnership used the university's College of Design (a cross-disciplinary school that helps shape presentations and functions in various venues) to facilitate a "design studio process." Over a two-day period, the team developed a common vision of an optimal school leader and the strategies needed to build that leader.

Three partnerships did not develop leader standards from scratch. Rather, they adapted or adopted state or national

---

Box 2.1
North Carolina State University's Team Engaged in a Collaborative Design Studio Process to Develop Leader Standards

The UPPI leadership team at NC State used the university's College of Design to facilitate a "design studio process." Over a two-day period, the team developed a common vision of an optimal school leader and strategies to build that leader—and the design experts created a graphic representation:

> We just sat in a room, and we're split up into groups, and [the design facilitators] gave us questions. There was chart paper everywhere. We talked about what a principal needed to be able to do, and we spent all day doing different things with that. . . . The next day, [we] had other similar activities [about] challenges and opportunities. Again tons of chart paper, tons of group work. [The] first draft . . . was pretty powerful to see.

Partners reported that the resulting visual clearly captured their perspectives and that they referenced it frequently in their work.

standards (i.e., PSEL). One partnership used its districts' standards, which are influenced by its state's requirements, to develop its program-level standards. Whether the program developed its own leader standards or adopted existing standards did not seem to affect how useful the standards were for the ensuing program redesign work.

Aligning existing program standards to state and national standards helped identify gaps in both the program standards and the state or national standards. As part of the process, all UPPI leadership teams performed a crosswalk of existing program standards to various external standards, including their state standards, and PSEL and NELP standards, at the request of and with support from The Wallace Foundation. This helped the programs identify gaps in their program standards. For example, the crosswalk revealed to two teams that their program paid insufficient attention to equity. Subsequently, the teams worked to ensure that equity was featured in their new set of program leader standards.

Each UPPI leadership team also completed a crosswalk of the baseline curriculum scope and sequence to their newly developed or adapted program standards. Thereafter, teams used the agreed-upon program standards as a benchmark against which to assess developments in the redesigned curriculum scope and sequence (i.e., once new course materials were drafted, programs again evaluated alignment to their program standards).

Some program teams struggled to balance program-specific and broader standards. One UL acknowledged the benefit of developing/adapting program-specific standards but also saw the limitation of these standards given the need for programs to meet state requirements and for districts to meet other state standards for administrators:

> I have such a mixed mind on this. So, each of the principal prep programs that I interacted with last week developed their own standards and they have state standards. So, I kept thinking, why are they developing their own . . . [w]hen they must show their accreditation to the state standards, which have been approved by the state.

In other words, to some, state standards will always be the defining expectations programs are held accountable to, and so it is unclear why it is important to develop separate, program-specific standards. Another university administrator recognized the necessity of overlapping standards from different agencies (e.g., state, districts), but identified as a challenge the amount of time required to ensure alignment to all sets of standards that programs and their partner districts are held accountable to.

Quality Measures Supported Program Assessment and Partnership-Building

QM is a tool that the Education Development Center (2009, 2018) developed, with support from The Wallace Foundation, to help principal preparation program leaders and others to assess the quality of pre-service principal training on six domains (candidate admissions, course content, pedagogy-andragogy, clinical practice, performance assessment, and graduate outcomes). QM is based on Darling-Hammond et al.'s (2007) research on exemplary principal preparation practices, and QM's rubric indicators and criteria, which describe effective practice, are linked with PSEL. UPPI teams were guided to use QM early in the partnership and to involve the district partners in the QM review. Teams followed the QM protocol, which, for most, meant having program faculty and district partners gather evidence to support preliminary ratings for each domain and convening to review evidence and agree upon ratings. According to the toolkit, the process would take at least one and a half days, usually spread over multiple sittings. Teams engaged in this once on their own, and a second time with the assistance of EDC facilitators.

QM supported reflection and relationship-building. Most ULs and their partners, including the district, state, and mentor program, described the QM exercise as a foundational experience that helped partners learn about one another's organizations and perspectives and facilitated relationship-building. For example, one district partner described QM as helping the partners to "build a common language" because "[the QM exercise] created a lot of questions about specific words that were used." The district and state interviewees perceived QM as particularly valuable in supporting non-university partners' understanding of the current program and the university perspective more broadly.

QM was a useful first step in self-assessment, but additional work was needed. Most ULs believed that QM helped their teams identify gaps and areas of strength in the current program, although some ULs felt that the insights generated through QM were not specific enough to support program improvement. Most ULs described QM as either having helped programs identify a need to collect additional evidence and engage in more self-reflection or as a useful starting point of a broader effort to collect additional evidence to support in-depth self-assessment. One UL described the process as "rough around the edges" but felt that it was "very informative" in that it helped the team understand where they needed to collect more data and how to begin the process of course redesign.

Program Logic Models Underpinned the Redesign Work and Contributed to Team-Building

In the first year of UPPI, each partnership developed a program-specific logic model showing its vision for how the redesign features they plan under UPPI will lead to the graduates they envision. Early in the project, The Wallace Foundation asked each partnership to undertake this task, believing that developing and using a sound logic model would drive the programs toward deeper change and stronger programs.

UPPI leadership teams tended to follow the same steps to develop their logic models. These steps included identifying goals for the redesigned program, identifying program features needed to meet these goals, assembling the collective thinking into a model, and making iterative revisions.

UPPI teams began by identifying goals for the redesign, drawing on their leader standards, conceptual frameworks, and theories of action. All this information fed into the team's logic model. Generally, most partnerships reported that reaching agreement on the goals of the redesign was easy and that they could reach consensus in almost every area. Focusing first on the outcomes and then on the path to reach those outcomes appeared to build a common commitment to resolve differences. As one UL noted, "There wasn't much disagreement; we all agreed on the outcomes. It's like we all were looking at this with the end in mind." Mentor programs helped facilitate the brainstorming sessions for some partnerships.

However, because partners did have different needs and perspectives, this process of developing a meaningful logic model and fully engaging partners was time-consuming. One UL noted that there was consensus on most of the work but that some areas were more sensitive. For example, the district and university partners might both want to align staff evaluation or hiring criteria to the logic model, but need union approval to make those changes. Despite such challenges in implementation, the partners did not disagree—they had built an understanding of each other. As one partner described, "It was this beautiful process of all of us evolving together."

The teams did wrestle with how to visually represent their logic models; this is consistent with substantial ambiguity in the literature on logic models, suggesting no single clear vision. Having a clear vision of the end product at the outset might have reduced some frustration in the process.

The process of developing logic models supported team-building. Building logic models supported team-building by helping all partners understand the entire initiative and how the pieces worked together. As noted by one UL,

> It was a very cathartic experience for the team, and I think everybody who was in the room [agreed]. . . . Everybody had pieces of [the initiative] that they knew were happening . . . but the majority of us had never seen the initiative . . . in its largest sense.

Box 2.2
UPPI Logic Models

What is a logic model? A logic model depicts and describes "the sequence of events thought to bring about benefits or change over time" (University of Wisconsin Extension School, 2002) and provides "stakeholders with a road map describing the sequence of related events" (W.K. Kellogg Foundation Evaluation Handbook, 1998).

What did UPPI logic models look like? Each site developed a core logic model depicting the program's redesign work with the engagement of its partners. Sites' logic models included many common components: resources (What do I need?), activities (What do I do?), outputs (What happens immediately?), and outcomes (What are my goals?) (Daugherty, Herman, and Unlu, 2017).

UPPI Logic models took on many different forms but many had some form of the features as illustrated in Figure 2.1.

Figure 2.1
Common Features of UPPI Redesign Logic Models

RESOURCES Organizations and materials	**ACTIVITIES** Key redesign tasks and strategies	**OUTPUTS** The redesigned program	**OUTCOMES** Intended impact
• UPPI project team • Partner organizations • Other state and national groups • Nonprofit organizations • Technical assistance providers • Leader standards	• Design curriculum and instruction • Develop clinical experiences • Establish more rigorous recruitment and selection processes • Coordinate activities around the leader tracking system	• UPPI program materials • Effective staff • Aligned curriculum • A leader tracking system	Some participants emphasized the development of transformational leaders or aimed for a model principal preparation program; others provided outcomes relevant to each partner (e.g., improved credentialing program or hiring practices)

What did it take to develop the UPPI logic model? Each partnership developed its logic model through an iterative process that involved input from its UPPI leadership team members. District and some state partners, for example, participated in brainstorming components of the model and in providing feedback on drafts. Partnerships drew on a variety of sources to develop the logic model, including conceptual frameworks of the most important components for program design, theories of action related to their core values and beliefs, and national, state, and local professional standards for school leaders. In most cases, the mentor program supported the development process by sharing their logic models and related documents.

According to another team, the logic model "helped us to refine our thinking, but also [gave] us a[n] heuristic. . . . This is how these are all interconnected and interrelate."

Further, in developing the logic model, the partners had an opportunity to share their thinking and be heard. This resulted in both a commitment to engage in the work and a logic model that reflected the perspectives of the stakeholders. As a respondent of one partnership noted,

> We can't only do things internally [within our organization]. We need to make sure that our partners understand our thinking and then can contribute their thinking. And then collectively come to these agreements so that everybody is, really, not just agreeing on the final product, but part of the process.

For example, districts of one partnership did not express ownership of the logic models or engage in its development initially. Over time, the districts' engagement in the logic models improved as the districts became more comfortable pushing their program partner to more clearly involve them, by asking, "Where are your districts in this?" The UL welcomed this nudge and the districts' perspective.

Being involved in the logic model development was also motivational for teams. It was a "celebration of how far we've come in such a short time," and it inspired teams to push harder. One respondent noted, "We came away thinking . . . we've done so much, but we have so much . . . to do. The logic model uncovers more."

Summary

Although all the UPPI leadership teams began the redesign with some evidence-aligned features and a plan for redesign, re-envisioning activities in the first year provided an opportunity to deepen their vision, better understand the areas of strength and where development was needed, unpack the relationships between their vision and status, and develop the partnerships needed to carry out the work. In the chapters that follow, we describe the programmatic changes that occurred in the first year and how the UPPI teams managed the work and built the partnerships.

CHAPTER THREE

Redesign of Program Features

The re-envisioning work discussed in the previous chapter created the platform for redesigning the program. Each UPPI program initially focused on redesigning its curriculum (i.e., courses of study, including the content and organization of courses). Beginning with the curriculum was a modification from the original proposed plan for some programs that had wanted to tackle clinical experience redesign first, but most respondents realized that it was appropriate to start with curriculum to drive fundamental program redesign. Some respondents, however, noted that a coherent, standards-aligned program must address all aspects of the learning experience together; as such, they also began work on redesigning clinical experience and recruitment and selection in the first year.

This chapter explores the redesign of curriculum, clinical experience, candidate recruitment and selection process, and related challenges and mitigating strategies.

Curriculum Redesign

As described earlier, UPPI programs had already been implementing some evidence-based practices and had taken a close look at the programs to identify areas for further development; the current goals were to align the curriculum to evidence-based standards, build program coherence, bridge theory and practice, promote active learning, and integrate district needs and perspectives. Each UPPI leadership team began with a guiding vision of its redesigned curriculum that revolved around incorporating more experiential learning and practice opportunities, essentially a guiding vision that tempered a traditional focus on theory. Some UPPI leadership teams prioritized tailoring the curriculum to their partner districts' needs. Overall, the curriculum redesign process was characterized by common activities and processes and facilitated greatly by faculty engagement.

Curriculum revision was in progress throughout the first year of UPPI; none of the universities had plans to start implementing a fully redesigned curriculum before spring 2018 at the earliest. Therefore, changes being considered have not been finalized; still, some early themes have emerged.

Program curricula had some common and some distinct features at baseline.
Programs embarked on curriculum changes from different starting points. While there
is not a standard curriculum for school leadership programs across the nation, professional standards and district expectations for school leaders drive programs toward
some common features. At baseline, the required courses among the seven programs
had some commonalities:

- Six programs appeared to have a course dedicated to school law and governance.
- Six programs had one or more courses focused on operations and management
  aspects of principalship.
- Five programs had a standalone course on instructional leadership.
- Five programs had a course dedicated to community relations.
- Four programs had a course focused on school improvement.
- Four programs included courses on research methods.
- Four programs had a course on professional learning and developing the potential
  in others.

However, there were also areas of difference, with programs offering courses that
were not found elsewhere. For example, one program had a course focused on educational technology. Moreover, the sequence of courses varied. For three of the six
programs with a course on school law, for example, such a course was among the first
in the program of study; for the other three programs, the course was offered later in
the course sequence. At least one program began with courses on operations and management (e.g., resource allocation), culminating in topics related to school improvement and transforming school culture, while another program led with a course on
leading school improvement. Accordingly, each of the seven UPPI leadership teams
identified various ways to redesign its program's curriculum. Many of these planned
changes emerged from the process of ensuring alignment of the redesigned program
with evidence-based standards. For instance, many teams identified a need to place
more deliberate emphasis on equity, which is a focus of PSEL.

Curriculum changes pointed toward more coherent programs. All programs
aimed to develop greater program coherence. Strategies to achieve this included building on core constructs across courses, developing assessments of cross-course assignments, and developing a tighter alignment between courses and clinical experiences.
For example, one UPPI leadership team organized its curriculum scope and sequence
around "competency projects or core assessments" and was working on revising the
key assessments to improve their rigor and alignment to the standards. Another team
created formative assessments each year, to review learning across courses, and a final,
summative exhibition of leadership and learning. Some teams have also considered
module and/or workshop formats of greater intensity for delivering curriculum. The
module format provides greater flexibility in terms of when to address a topic and more

coherence in the curriculum if modules are designed to align with concurrent internship experiences.

UPPI leadership teams identified potential changes to course offering and scope and sequence to address gaps. Upon conducting program self-assessment and alignment activities (e.g., performing crosswalks of syllabi to national and state professional standards), all teams identified gaps in course offerings or course content. The actual gaps and plans for revision appeared site-specific, dependent on what the state of the program at baseline. For example, two teams determined that they needed to better prepare candidates to take on the role of an administrator from the outset of the program; having been teachers, candidates tended to have a good foundation for the instructional leadership aspect, but they needed content and experiences around budget and operations. Another team realized that its program addressed teaching and learning well, but not skills around developing relationships and building culture and climate. Yet another team identified a need to focus additional attention on special education through the redesign. Details about how any of the planned changes will manifest (e.g., whether there will be a dedicated course on special education or whether it will be integrated among other courses) were not yet available at the end of the first year of the redesign.

UPPI leadership teams sought to incorporate adult learning theory and use more interactive instructional techniques. Some teams emphasized applying adult education theory and research in redesigning the instructional approach. These teams explicitly recognized the potentially different learning needs of their adult students as compared with undergraduate and younger learners. For example, adult learners may be more intrinsically motivated; they bring a wealth of prior experiences that can be activated, and they may be more able to engage in critical reflection. Teams also discussed (greater) use of interactive instructional techniques. In fact, UPPI teams at four of the seven universities expressed a desire to make learning more interactive and practice-based for candidates. In particular, teams considered incorporating more class discussion, role plays, and simulations of real decisionmaking scenarios for candidates to navigate.

UPPI leadership teams recognized a need to balance theory and practice. One aspect that each team considered in its redesign plans is the balance between theory and practice in its curriculum. Many district partners suggested that curricula be updated with current and lived knowledge from the field, stemming from concern that some professors "haven't been in schools in years, and . . . depending on their level of interest and learning, haven't really updated their knowledge and skills." Meanwhile, some research faculty initially voiced concerns about incorporating more practical applications (e.g., how to constructively deliver negative performance reviews) alongside research and theory (e.g., components of a learning culture) in the curriculum. The perspectives were not unbridgeable, however. As one district lead noted:

We have to be willing to accept the research-based philosophies that universities can bring to us. We tend to focus on practice, policy, and politics. We know some best practices and I feel good about what we're doing, but it doesn't mean they're research-based . . .

In most partnerships, team members came to acknowledge that the tension between theory and practice was likely to remain and is perhaps essential to a well-designed program and to the redesign process. As one faculty member said:

I think there's a tension, and not a fight tension, but a tension like on the road between practitioner and theorist, and that tension needs to be there and it has to give back and forth.

In terms of strategies to balance theory and practice, one team's goal for program redesign was to better contextualize theory or abstractions from a practitioner's perspective. To do this, it sought to orient the curriculum and assessments around the actual experiences and activities of today's school principals, with the goal of ensuring that candidates left the program with a set of frameworks that would allow them to more adeptly navigate challenges in school leadership. Second, most teams explicitly recognized the importance of having instructors with current real-world school leadership experiences. Teams generally wanted to provide principal candidates the ability to "hit the ground running in their roles." Being able to do this largely depends on the candidate's knowledge of what school leadership really entails and what problems of practice to expect. As one respondent said, "We want to . . . bring that real-life work that's going on in the district into [the classroom]." Some programs already use partner district staff as instructors, and others are moving in that direction.

UPPI leadership teams actively sought to understand district partners' perspectives and needs and to address them in the redesigned curriculum. To collect such information and feedback from the district partners, most teams leveraged standing UPPI leadership team meetings. Further, they have invited sitting administrators from the partner districts to join meetings to share their perspectives as current prin-

---

Box 3.1
Steps in an Example Curriculum Redesign Process

During the first year of UPPI, the curriculum redesign work was typically delegated to a curriculum redesign task force. Across sites, ULs and task force members reported performing some common steps, as follows:

1. Develop program leader standards. Complete a crosswalk exercise that maps program leader standards onto state standards and onto the national PSEL standards to identify gaps, and then revise standards accordingly.
2. Use the early conceptual work—including findings from the QM exercise, the logic model, and the program leader standards—to develop a draft curriculum scope and sequence.
3. Distribute draft curriculum scope and sequence throughout partnerships and potential other stakeholders for review. Concurrently, strategize (university faculty and the UL) to identify the most effective and expedient approach to implement proposed changes through university institutional processes.

cipals. Finally, some teams conducted interviews or a survey to help gain insights into district needs and to generate ideas for district-tailored course content.

Practitioner perspectives on the work of school leaders and problems of practice in the field helped inform critical areas traditionally under-addressed or missing from principal preparation programs. One district lead, for example, pointed out that the parent and community engagement piece and issues around student discipline are critical to the real life that a school leader lives, but are often neglected in preparation programs. Superintendents and practicing principals also noted that candidates need more training and development with respect to communication. As one UL reported, "When we talked about this with our superintendents and people practicing in the field, we even did a survey of practicing principals about . . . what were most important [skills] and . . . across the board . . . it was communication, that new principals have got to know how to communicate with teachers, with stakeholders, with parents, with superintendents. There's got to be that explicit focus on communication." Finally, another district lead reported that, directly as a result of their involvement in the curriculum redesign, the revised program will emphasize "cultural responsiveness and how [to] respond to specific needs of a very diverse population of students."

Clinical Experience

All UPPI leadership teams recognized the importance of clinical experiences for their principal candidates and expressed a commitment to enhancing this aspect of their programs. The programs aimed to give candidates a variety of practical, on-the-ground experiences to help them understand what a school administrator does day-to-day. They also thought about how to assess clinical learning. One team member described it this way:

> [W]e really focused on what are the practical experiences . . . what they will look like[?] How are you going to assess that they have not just the knowledge about finance per se, but [that] they have the skills to manage a budget within their building?

Although it was early in the process of redesigning the clinical experiences, the teams explored the following changes toward evidence-based practices: (1) aligning clinical experiences with standards and curriculum, (2) providing candidates with realistic principal experiences, (3) extending the length of the clinical experience, and (4) considering options for enhancing the mentoring, supervision, and evaluation of candidates during the clinical experience.

UPPI leadership teams sought to align clinical experiences with standards and curriculum. In redesigning their clinical experience component, teams considered alignment with program and professional standards. Such alignment can be an especially difficult part of clinical redesign because external partners and bureaucracies are often essential for successful alignment. In the case of clinical redesign, most teams reported that state partners were directly involved in shaping the clinical component and establishing state requirements such as certification tests or minimum clinical experience hours. In the case of Florida, a 2017 state law (enacted independent of UPPI) requires universities and districts to deeply collaborate on parameters of the principal candidate's clinical experience. In addition to state standards, some teams were also considering national standards in their clinical experience redesign. For example, one team was working with its mentor program to integrate University Council for Educational Administration (UCEA) guidelines on clinical practice.

UPPI leadership teams also aimed to align clinical experiences with the redesigned curriculum when possible. At baseline, the types and timing of clinical experiences students had were often dependent on the school-based mentor principal; course topics and practical experiences rarely intentionally connected and reinforced each other. Moving forward, some teams plan to explore ways to better cohere the two core program components.

UPPI leadership teams were working to provide candidates with experiences that represent the work of real principals. Nearly all teams explicitly recognized that to develop practical knowledge and skills, candidates needed opportunities to engage in hands-on activities that reflect the duties of a principal. In place of interviewing or passively shadowing a sitting principal, or serving as "another set of hands to handle discipline or some other menial administrative task," for example, candidates would benefit from writing and implementing a school improvement plan. This might involve providing professional learning to teachers, monitoring implementation and progress, and engaging stakeholders. Importantly, candidates need opportunities to provide instructional leadership, for example, through conducting observations of teaching and providing effective feedback. If timed appropriately, candidates can also be involved in planning for school-year opening or be included in budget conversations. As one district lead said, "Anything experiential and project-based is going to be probably more worthwhile to the candidate because they are really digging in and rolling up their sleeves and doing the work as opposed to reading about the work or talking about the work." Perhaps most ideally, candidates would have the opportunity to authentically experience the "principal's seat" through an internship, where they would have to manage multiple priorities and responsibilities and make strategic decisions.

UPPI leadership teams explored options for extending the clinical experience to better develop principal candidates. At baseline, programs' clinical experience requirements ranged from having candidates complete course-embedded assignments at their own school in nonteaching hours, to yearlong, full-time clinical experiences. As part of the redesign, teams aimed to provide extended clinical opportunities. By one team's account, clinical experience would ideally be like an apprenticeship in which candidates work with principals strategically and intensely. In this respect, one option some teams explored was requiring a yearlong but part-time clinical experience. While the experience would be part-time, it would give candidates a strong understanding of the work of a principal from the beginning to the end of a school year. Part-time interns, however, tend to be assigned specific duties, such as bus duty (termed "random acts of administration" by one respondent) and to carry out self-designed projects. Another, more ideal, option a few sites explored was to offer yearlong, full-time clinical experiences. During such experiences, candidates have the opportunity to address the types of problems that occur frequently on the job.

UPPI leadership teams acknowledged that clinical experiences closer to true apprenticeships implied greater program costs. Such high costs are a major obstacle, particularly for districts. This is because most principal candidates are employed full-time in their teaching position while attending a principal preparation program. Intense, full-time apprenticeships during the regular workday would require a source of funding for principal candidates and/or staff hired to replace them. One program that had received state funding to run a full-time, yearlong clinical experience had to end this opportunity after state budget cuts; it was infeasible for the program and districts to sustain. Another potential burden of full-time, extended clinical experiences is that they may require rearranging preparation program courses to evenings and/or weekends so that principal candidates could commit more time to in-school activities and tasks. Overall, funding and other attendant issues complicate the intent many programs have to bring full-time, yearlong internship experiences to principal candidates.

UPPI leadership teams considered ways to improve mentoring, supervision, and evaluation in the clinical experiences. Candidates are supervised in the field by practicing school or district leaders. A respondent emphasized the general importance of the field-based supervisor (called a mentor principal at some programs), saying, "The quality of the mentor principal is probably the most significant variable to student success outside of the curriculum itself." However, some mentor principals assumed that important role by virtue of being principals in schools where the candidate was teaching, and thus did not always have the interest, time, or skills to be a strong, engaged mentor. UPPI leadership teams explored strategies to strengthen the mentoring component, such as training mentor principals for their role or limiting the mentor role to principals who are themselves highly effective and who intentionally take on the mentor responsibilities.

Typically, candidates in the field are also supervised by university-based program staff. The role of these supervisors is also being reexamined. First, most teams realized that the ability of these supervisors to provide meaningful feedback depends partly on the amount of time they can devote to each candidate. Most supervisors have limited time, either because they have other roles in their institutions or an overwhelming number of candidates to supervise. Some teams have recognized that the quality of the interactions between supervisors and candidates also requires reconsideration. To this end, a few teams further along in their clinical experience redesign have already decided to move from the supervision model to a coaching model. One program faculty described supervision as "somewhat compliance-oriented"; supervisors perform rather perfunctory "check-ins" with each candidate, monitoring to make sure that students are participating in required experiences. In contrast, coaching is more interactive and attentive to individual candidates' needs. It is designed to help each candidate move along in his or her continuum of development as a future principal. Compared with supervision, coaching is more labor-intensive and less evaluative in nature. Programs planning to move to coaching planned to train their university-based supervisors (and possibly also field-based supervisors/mentors) in this new role.

Candidate Recruitment and Selection

Curriculum redesign efforts led all teams to reflect to some degree on their recruitment and selection processes. The ideas they explored were largely consistent with effective practices of actively recruiting highly qualified candidates and using performance-based assessments to select the best candidates. Most teams aimed to become more selective. In addition to selecting individuals that have the skills, abilities, and experiences needed to succeed in the program, teams sought to select applicants that aspire to be school leaders, not applicants seeking the degree or certification for a salary increase or with the intent of taking on other administrative roles (e.g., program coordinator, manager of school or district fiscal services).

Selectivity had potentially important implications for program operations. Most UPPI leadership teams recognized a need to maintain or enhance the diversity of the candidate pool on multiple demographic dimensions, including gender, race, and ethnicity. Some teams expressed concerns about being able to attract a large enough candidate pool to maintain diversity with more stringent selection criteria in place. On the whole though, UPPI teams were committed to maintaining and even enhancing the diversity represented by their candidates as they worked to establish more selective criteria. One team further noted that being more selective may result in shrinking cohort size, which may pose fiscal problems; that is, the program would like to be more selective, but securing tuition dollars is a priority that cannot be overlooked. Although some ULs referenced the idea that the university would likely favor the income generated by a larger, less selective program, this assumption did not appear to influence the early thinking around setting more rigorous selection criteria.

At the end of the first year of the initiative, most UPPI leadership teams were still planning changes to candidate recruitment and selection processes. Only one or two teams have made definite and significant changes to principal candidate recruitment and selection processes. To date, teams planned to use two related levers in their efforts to enhance candidate selectivity—district input and more in-depth, performance-based assessments. Teams' strategies for enhancing district input in candidate selection included placing district superintendents on the candidate selection committee, requiring district leaders' recommendation for admittance, and revising candidate performance assessments based on district input. In addition, most teams were interested in using intensive performance-based tasks in candidate selection. At a minimum, such tasks include writing samples and/or analyses of their current school operations and performance. More intensive performance-based tasks include in-person, sometimes daylong, interviews with ad hoc scenario analyses and other interactive tasks simulating the work of principals.

Challenges and Mitigating Strategies

While UPPI leadership teams have made a significant amount of progress with program redesign in the first year of the initiative, they also encountered several common program redesign challenges. These pertained to (1) innovating within traditional university guidelines, (2) aligning curriculum with multiple sets of standards, and (3) balancing district-specific needs with more general needs. With most of these challenges, teams have developed mitigation strategies.

Traditional university structures challenged the adoption of innovative approaches. A significant source of tension that UPPI leadership teams identified was trying to develop an innovative approach to curriculum structure and delivery while working within traditional university guidelines that tended to limit innovation. For example, some teams proposed creating one-credit-hour modules in lieu of three-credit-hour courses to provide programs with more flexibility over the course scope and sequence, but this proposal could have implications for faculty meeting their course load obligations. Similarly, some teams wanted to shift some teaching responsibilities to adjunct or clinical faculty instead of full-time research faculty, which would have consequences for university program staffing.

Across partnerships, partners reported that the UL and/or those with deepest institutional knowledge helped to navigate the institutional context. In practice, ULs approached the challenges noted above by becoming familiar with the full range of flexibilities and options within the university to identify the most appropriate, and often expedient, avenue to achieve the initiative's goal. For example, one team made revisions that did not require changing the course names and numbers; only courses where the names and numbers change are required to go through the university course approval process. In a few instances, the ULs relied on experience gained through previous redesign work and long tenures within their institutions.

Faculty of some programs were disengaged in the redesign work. In some teams, early on, faculty members were reportedly resistant to curriculum and program change and to engaging in UPPI. Some UPPI leadership teams faced resistance rooted in very real apprehensions about the direction of the redesign. In these few teams, faculty felt that the redesign implicated too much change too quickly. They were concerned, for example, about potentially shifting to more online courses or losing the theoretical piece of leadership development in their courses in order to make room for more practice-based applications. Compounding, or perhaps underlying, these concerns seemed to be some faculty concern with potentially losing ownership of a program they had helped develop or courses they had helped craft and become accustomed to delivering. In line with this, some university and district staff perceived that tenured faculty did not have the experience—or sometimes the interest—to teach in a hands-on, practice-based, and experiential way.

Teams approached the faculty disengagement issues in different ways. To help alleviate faculty resistance to change and signal that their concerns are valid and ideas welcome, one UPPI team worked to establish a more welcoming environment for faculty, engaging them in more redesign-related activities and inviting faculty to key UPPI events. Another team focused on helping prepare faculty for likely shifts in program pedagogy and content, for example, by offering faculty some professional development around best practices on instructing adult learners through experiential and problem-based learning.

Other UPPI leadership teams faced faculty pushback for more operational reasons—specifically, tenured faculty expressed that they had limited time to engage in the redesign and already juggled competing priorities. Indeed, respondents of most teams noted securing faculty release time to work on the redesign was a barrier. Some faculty members have taken the initiative to request release time. To attempt to minimize the burden or expectation on the faculty, one program director assigned faculty members manageable and concrete components of tasks to work on and offered departmental time for them to engage in the redesign work. Some other teams leaned more on practitioners or adjuncts to make progress on certain tasks.

Summary

The first year of UPPI was primarily spent on re-envisioning the program and redesigning the curriculum. The curriculum redesign thus far has reflected the importance of both theory and practice; teams have adopted new research-based leader standards and incorporated input from district partners on real problems of practice that principals experience on the job. All teams are still working through the other components of the redesign, such as clinical experience and candidate recruitment and selection. Across teams, common priorities have emerged across components of the redesign. One primary priority is to build a more coherent program, in which curriculum, instruction, and clinical experiences align with each other, with the program standards, and with state and national standards. A second priority is to integrate theory and practice and to capitalize on district partners' contributions to create a more practice-centered program that addresses districts' needs. UPPI leadership teams have also expressed the importance of university faculty buy-in to ensure the future and ongoing implementation of the program redesign.

CHAPTER FOUR

Leadership of the Redesign Process

Dedicated and effective leadership has been recognized as a key feature of exemplary principal preparation programs. Darling-Hammond et al. (2007) reported that such programs benefited from leaders "who had the vision, commitment, and capacity to coordinate stakeholders, secure resources, and implement critical features well" (p. 147). The experience of the UPPI programs illustrates the importance of effective leadership, not only for the programs but for their redesign as well. This chapter provides some emerging findings about the practices that seem effective in pushing the redesign work forward. While the report as a whole focuses on trends across the seven sites, this chapter features text boxes highlighting a specific practice at each site that supported the redesign process.

University-Based Leads Played a Critical Role Across All Sites

The UL is the individual from each university leading the overall redesign effort at each of the seven sites. All of the ULs are part of the school of education. Two ULs are heads or chairs of the departments housing the principal preparation programs. Two other ULs are directors or coordinators of the program under redesign. One is interim dean, and two sites have assistant or associate professors serving in the role of UL.

ULs provided commitment, ownership, enthusiasm, and time to keep the work moving forward. Other respondents mentioned ULs' level of organization, dedication (both in time and energy), and success in bringing people

> **Box 4.1**
> **University of Connecticut's Project Lead Generated Buy-In Within the Department for the Program Redesign**
>
> The UL at UCONN used skills he gleaned from leadership experience and training to garner interest and buy-in with professors in the Department of Educational Leadership who are not core to the UPPI effort. The department houses UCONN's Administrator Preparation Program (UCAPP), the program under redesign, and some professors in the department teach courses for this as well as other programs. To generate support for the redesign, for example, the UL ensured that the professors received all products prior to public release. The UL also held one-on-one meetings with faculty members to provide them with essential information about the effort. Establishing a group of informed faculty members in the department was designed to help disseminate the message and make the redesign process more transparent for all faculty.

together and building relationships as key facilitators for the work. ULs reportedly used their influence and relationships to ensure that the right people were engaged and buying into the initiative from the beginning and throughout as needs arose. They were also often instrumental in developing and securing superintendent and university administrator buy-in early in the initiative. Most of the programs' partners pointed to strong management skills—for example, establishing timelines and meeting norms—and effective communication as the major UL contributions in managing the redesign.

Redesign Work Requires a Strategic Perspective and Operational Capacity

The redesign work is a complex endeavor that entails interfacing with broader activities in several different organizations, all of which have their own objectives. Accomplishing the work requires collaboration among individuals within each organization who have a strategic perspective and with those who have the operational capacity to execute the work. The strategic perspective is needed to provide a vision of how each organization aims to influence or be influenced by the effort, to ensure organizational commitment to the initiative, and to ensure alignment between the program redesign and the broader vision and priorities of the organizations. Individuals filling this strategic role included the dean and UL at the university, the superintendent or assistant superintendent from the districts, and director-level positions at state departments of education or other state entity. To complement the strategic perspective, most partner organizations also engaged someone who could operationalize these visions into deliverables. Examples of individuals who filled this role were directors of leadership development at the districts, adjunct or clinical faculty members at the universities, and program specialists or consultants at the state departments of education or other state entity.

Depending on the size and capacity of the partner organizations, one or multiple individuals served in these two roles. Most universities had at least one person primarily in a strategic role and one person primarily in an operational role. For smaller partner organizations and districts, one person often served in both the strategic and operational roles. However, in some of those partner organizations, it was somewhat difficult to

> **Box 4.2**
> **Virginia State University Used Continual Communication and Co-Development to Build Capacity**
>
> VSU built strategic and operational capacity across the team by calling on every team member to participate in activities on both strategic and operational levels. District partners, who were engaged in co-designing the project at the proposal stage, helped keep the team focused on the redesign themes during staffing transitions. VSU faculty, who stayed current on the initiative through regular UPPI meetings, were able to take on one another's tasks as needed. Even when the state partner and mentor program did not have specific roles, they participated in redesign meetings and activities and were able to identify places where they could contribute. This investment of time in training and communication has helped the VSU team maintain direction during periods of transition.

move the UPPI work forward because the workload for the individual became overwhelming. Over time, other staff (e.g., district members) were brought on board to provide support, particularly operational support. Those organizations that needed additional operational support hired new staff members or drew upon administrative project staff and/or graduate assistants.

In some cases, the role of the ULs themselves changed from one that was more operational initially to one that was more strategic after hiring additional operations staff. The ULs' role was very time-consuming, and engaging in operational work on an ongoing basis limited some ULs' availability to provide strategic leadership. For example, some ULs initially engaged in the operational task of setting up the working groups and subcommittees. Once those structures were successfully implemented, they put in place operational staff to lead the committees, thus freeing up the UL to engage with university, district, and state leadership to clear hurdles for implementation and begin thinking about the initiative's sustainability. One UL reflected on his changing role after he hired more operational staff:

> My role kind of has become more of a higher-level overseer as opposed to [one of] being down in the weeds. . . . Getting all these other positions has given me the ability to not have to [worry] about the weeds. The project as [it] gets bigger, it means that you do need a more of a bird's eye view of what's going on.

By design, UPPI partnerships call for district leadership to actively engage in shaping the preparation programs to ensure that the programs meet district needs. It appeared important to ensure that district partners included individuals that played a strategic vision–setting role in their organization. In two cases where the district partners did not have the involvement of their leaders (e.g., superintendents or assistant superintendents), the ULs were concerned that the initiative would not reflect the districts' priorities and might not be sustained. For example, one UL initiated check-in calls twice a month with each of the three superintendents to ensure that the superintendents agreed with the changes being made with the redesign so that there would be continued support for the initiative beyond the duration of UPPI.

Strategic engagement took on a slightly different form for participating UPPI districts that were a part of a consortium of districts. Each consortium had a coordinator, or lead, who played a crucial role in managing operational and logistical matters for their member districts. For example, these consortium leads scheduled meetings and managed communication, thereby freeing the district representatives to focus on substantive issues. They drew on member districts for input. For example, one consortium lead attended UPPI leadership team meetings and then held separate meetings with member districts to deliberate and reach consensus on UPPI-related action items, such as approving revised curriculum and standards. This approach reportedly worked well. Because most of the districts in the consortium were small with limited staff capacity to dedicate to UPPI, the fact that a consortium lead handled operational matters allowed district staff to make substantive contributions. The consortium approach to involving districts provides smaller, rural districts with a collective voice in shaping the programs that prepare their principals, an opportunity they do not often have.

Key Strategic Approaches Helped Manage the Redesign Process

UPPI team leaders used several strategies to drive the redesign work: (1) building relationships and establishing a culture of trust and collaboration, (2) developing and maintaining a common goal, (3) "going slow to go fast," and (4) using the logic model to guide the work.

Building relationships and establishing a culture of trust and collaboration were essential to a smooth collaborative redesign process. Across all teams, there was a strong emphasis on building and nurturing relationships. Most teams recognized that openness, trust, and a culture of collaboration were essential for change management. One UL stated:

> I think that we're very comfortable to reach out to each other and have conversations, even courageous conversations at times, and that's important in change. If you can't have that relationship, that trust, and have the conversations, I don't think change occurs.

Positive relationships also supported informal conversations as needed (e.g., project leads texting each other while working on UPPI deliverables or talking during other, non-UPPI events).

Most ULs attributed improvement in the management of the redesign to growing trust and support between partners:

> I think what we will see are people being more and more honest, so as we go along, I think we will see the culture around this group will grow and change, and people will trust more and more. As they trust more, I think we will be able to have more honest work.

Nurturing, responsive relationships also meant understanding and accommodating partners' perspectives and circumstances. For example, at one program in which the district hiring timeline was different from the university program redesign timeline, the university was able to adjust the program redesign schedule so that districts could hire people to work on UPPI at the opportune time. In addition, ULs were sensitive to the amount of time that district leads had to work on UPPI, given their full-time positions at their districts.

One program interviewee emphasized that organizational culture, if not aligned among partners, can disrupt the change process. Multiple interviewees in both university and district roles have said, for example, that district staff are often concerned with practical applications of ideas and with achieving immediate results, whereas university faculty members often place more value on identifying or understanding the theory or conceptual framework that underlies practices. Growing a culture of collaboration, engagement, and passion is one strategy for combating such differences in culture.

Developing and maintaining a common goal kept the work moving forward. Most partnerships used and endorsed the backward-mapping approach of establishing a common vision and working backward from this vision to develop roles, responsibilities, and processes to reach their goals. The common vision expressed by most UPPI teams was to improve student achievement via effective school leaders; the teams began by clearly defining "effective school leaders," which was supported in part by development of leader standards and logic models at the start of the redesign. Most ULs managed the redesign by making common goals clear among all partner leads. In one case, the overarching goal of UPPI helped a district lead move the work forward in a more collaborative way:

> You have to remind yourself, how can I provide this feedback to the university so they can get information on how well their graduates are doing, and what else can I do as a district to help the university to meet their goals? It's very easy to box yourself off and think as a district. Make a conscientious effort not to do that. . . . I find myself . . . saying to my team and myself, "Remember now this is not just for [our district]."

"Going slow to go fast" was a difficult but valuable lesson for change management. This refers to the strategy of approaching tasks with great deliberation and intentionality rather than rushing to complete the tasks. The idea is that going at a slower pace helps to avoid mistakes or oversights and facilitates deeper conceptualization of the change and clearer vision of the end goal. While at one time or another, many project leads (both university- and district-based) have balked at the idea of going slow to go fast, finding it frustrating to not be able to accomplish as much as they had hoped in the first year, they evolved to appreciate the strategy.

With respect to building the leader tracking system (LTS), particular early on, some teams wondered why they could not just acquire or adapt an already developed system instead of beginning from scratch. Others thought they already had enough clarity to begin building one. Gradually, as they engaged in the work, however, teams realized that by discussing potential data points to track, they were strengthening their agreement about what to look for in an effective leader. Moreover, pausing to take stock of existing data and data sources helped them envision a more efficient system by not replicating existing efforts. Finally, developing a request for proposals (RFPs) from vendors forced teams to think about and articulate when and how the system will be used, by whom, and for what purposes. As one district lead said, "We were wanting to rush and get into it and do the work . . . but it has been a good process, and it has really kind of made us think about what is important and could be realistic." Another leader commented, "I definitely [agree with] the recommendation [of] not running out and buying an LTS program. You definitely have to map and go through this work."

Logic models helped develop common understanding by guiding the work and serving as a communication tool. The logic model played a role in guiding the redesign process by acting as a "road map" for the initiative: "We use the logic model as a roadmap. . . . It has been used to keep us on the body of work." As a reminder of that focus, one team used the logic model at the beginning of team meetings to ground the work of that meeting in the larger plan. Some teams mentioned that they used benchmarks in the logic models to check whether they were on track. Further, teams used the logic models to think through the repercussions of making changes in their redesigns. Because the logic models showed the relationships across various aspects of the redesign, teams could see how a change in one area of the redesign may necessitate changes in other areas. More than just a planning tool, some teams described the logic model as a "driver" of their work: "The logic model undergirds everything we do. . . . It drives the planning, it drives the administration, the monitoring, the data, etc."

Many of the UPPI leadership teams also used the logic model to communicate about their program externally with stakeholders, such as state-level organizations, principals, and the public, because it provided an overview of what the program is about in one snapshot. Several teams have used the logic model to brief new team members, such as new faculty. Another team provided the new interim dean the logic model to prepare her to discuss UPPI in a presentation. One state partner shared the logic model with its internal team working on developing a new school leader assessment for the state:

> At the meetings, the stakeholders would work on the assessment. The logic model has been a great way for us to explain to some of the stakeholders what the project's about and to explain what the other components are so they understand the project beyond just the assessment team, but the scope of all the other pieces working together to create sort of a cohesive system.

Then again, several respondents, mainly from districts, reported that they have not referred to the logic model since it was developed. For some, it was not concrete enough to guide the daily work. Other teams preferred to use other tools that were more useful, such as a wall map with outcomes listed by month. Still others indicated that they had moved beyond the need for a logic model: "We were already having those conversations without the logic model. It's not something we need a copy of. It's already embedded in what we were doing."

UPPI Leadership Teams Evolved Structures to Organize the Redesign Process

To effectively and efficiently manage a complex program redesign involving many different partners, it is crucial to establish sound structures. While all partnerships had a centralized UPPI leadership team, they differed in how they organized people to do the work and to collaborate on decisionmaking.

Having a core leadership team and regular meetings maintained continuity. All partnerships established a regular, formal UPPI leadership team and held regular meetings with representatives from each partner organization (university, district/consortium, state, and mentor program). Most teams used these meetings to work on specific tasks, whereas a few partnerships used these meetings primarily for progress updates. These meetings occurred as often as every two weeks, every three weeks, or every month. Some partnerships took time early in the initiative to co-construct meeting norms (e.g., be an active participant, all voices should be heard, be respectful, be fully attentive). Respondents from one partnership found that setting and revisiting norms improved engagement by minimizing undesirable behaviors, such as doing non-UPPI work during meetings. Agendas, minutes, and timelines were posted in common spaces and used to guide meetings.

Some teams specifically chose to meet in person, despite distance, to build rapport and focus on the work, while others prioritized convenience and were sensitive to how difficult it was for district partner leads to meet in person. Some teams took turns hosting the meetings, so that each partner had a chance to be visible. The partnerships that adopted this approach found that it increased levels of trust, engagement, and commitment and supported relationship-building. It also meant that partners shared the burden of travel and the time it took to attend meetings.

Two models of collaboration emerged, reflecting different contexts and opportunities. Some of the part-

> **Box 4.3**
> **Meeting Norms at Albany State University Played an Important Role**
> ASU's UPPI leadership took the time at the start of the initiative to set norms for the team for all meetings. The norms were meant to stress collegiality. They included such ideas as all partners should be active participants, all voices should be heard, partners should work as a group, and everyone should be respectful of one another. ASU's UL or a partner lead typically read the norms at the start of the team's meetings, and partners have been receptive to this practice. An additional related protocol the team adopted was for everyone to share a final thought (something they learned or viewed as important) at the end of each meeting.

> **Box 4.4**
> **San Diego State University's Meetings Created Partner Interdependence**
> SDSU holds in-person meetings with its UPPI partners every month. The in-person meetings have generated an increased level of trust between the partners. As one partner stated: "At the last meeting, one of the district leads said it's no longer collaboration, it's more like interdependence. Now, we can't imagine designing anything without the district partners on board. It's become a very deep and connected set of relationships." All the partners found the meetings to be productive, and they appreciated the agendas that are circulated in advance to help them keep on track.

nerships used a model best described as *co-development*, in which representatives from the university program and from each district worked together in subgroups to execute key redesign tasks (Figure 4.1). In this model, the districts were deeply engaged in the co-development process, for example, as active members of a curriculum work group. Typically in this model, the UL made the ultimate decision, with input from partners as needed.

In contrast, the model best described as *input and delegation* is characterized by a multistep process. First, district partner leads helped to conceptualize redesign features during UPPI leadership team meetings. Next, the ULs delegated the work to individuals or groups within a single organization (e.g., a group of university faculty or a single district person). Then, the work was brought back to the cross-organizational leadership team for review. In this model, districts were involved in framing and reviewing

Figure 4.1
Two Example Models of Collaboration

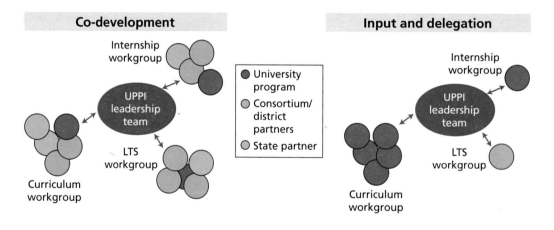

Box 4.5
Compare and Contrast: Curriculum Workgroups at Florida Atlantic University and the University of Connecticut

FAU *(co-development)*: The curriculum committee at FAU included faculty from FAU and adjunct faculty from each partner district. Initially, the FAU faculty met weekly to discuss the curriculum plan overall. Then, each faculty member was assigned a specific course and a team of adjunct faculty from the partner districts; each course redesign worked like small subcommittees within the committee—each set up its own meetings and was responsible for deliverables. Partners viewed this committee structure as a true collaboration.

UCONN *(input and delegation)*: The curriculum workgroup was led by a tenured faculty member. The workgroup members consisted of full-time faculty serving as instructors for the principal preparation program and select adjunct faculty members, all of whom were appointed to the work group. The workgroup did not include UPPI partner district leads. The group initially met monthly and then more frequently as it developed detailed plans. The group also broke into four smaller subcommittees in the summer—one for each of the four elements of the redesigned curriculum—to work on the specific courses within each element. Once the element plans were completed, the committee was put on hold, and the UL and two members of the UPPI leadership team took over the details of the curriculum work.

the work, but someone else, usually from the university, carried out the operational steps of the task.

District context, preference, and capacity played a role in the model of collaboration used in each partnership. In some cases, while districts may have appreciated the opportunity to work alongside the university program, as in the co-development model, because of the capacity limitations of the district leads, they were limited to providing input, as in the input and delegation model.

A Range of Resources Supported the Redesign Effort

UPPI leadership teams had access to a range of resources that supported the redesign effort. These supports included backing from the university administrators, expertise of the mentor programs, financial support from the UPPI grant, and opportunities to learn and share redesign ideas at professional learning community meetings.

University administrators supported the program redesign effort. Such support included offering flexibility in using resources, giving course buy-outs to the UL and key university staff involved in the redesign, providing dedicated UPPI work space, garnering buy-in from faculty members, speaking about the initiative at state and other gatherings, advocating up to senior university administrators, and making connections with key stakeholders. ULs considered such support instrumental in their being able to focus on the redesign and accomplish the work, and in knowing the work is valued and that administrators will help clear barriers if necessary (for example, during the course approval process). Absent some such support, however, ULs reported that the redesign would likely still progress, given the will of the UPPI leadership team and district partners. In fact, some ULs identified additional supports they would like to have had from university administrators, but have managed well without. These included more hands-on support in thought-partnering and decisionmaking around the redesign.

Mentor programs drew on their expertise to respond to university programs' needs. Some UPPI leadership teams required support with management of the redesign process. Mentor programs have helped by assisting with meeting preparation, facilitating meetings, and documenting the team's work. For other teams, the mentor program served as a thought partner to the university, which entailed guiding the UL and program faculty through the cycles of inquiry—an iterative process of taking in feedback, revising ideas, and re-examining them for further improvement. For these teams, the mentor programs created a feedback loop and provided an external perspective to the UPPI leadership team about what was going well and what needed attention in the partnership.

Mentor programs drew on the lessons learned from previous redesigns to guide the current work, either through discussions with the UL or with the full UPPI leadership team. For example, prior to UPPI, some mentor programs had assisted other districts in developing an LTS and were thus able to provide examples of these systems and suggestions for how to build them. With respect to the curriculum redesign component, most mentor programs provided input on the various work products developed in curriculum committees.

Mentor programs encouraged and assisted in the use of evidence-based approaches to assessing the strengths and weaknesses of the existing principal preparation programs prior to the redesign. This support involved developing data-collection tools and gathering data through interviews and focus groups of current district personnel and/or recent principal graduates. The approach has helped the UPPI leadership teams identify where to concentrate changes in their programs. For example, one mentor program conducted focus groups specifically to study shortcomings in the preparation of a program's existing clinical component. The UPPI leadership team plans to use that information to target features that need improvement when it begins redesigning the clinical experience.

Another mentor program specifically interviewed the district partners (e.g., district administrators and principals who graduated from the university's program) to learn about the existing district landscape with respect to principal preparation prior to the redesign. From these district scans, the university was able to identify components of its principal preparation program it can improve to better meet the needs of the districts.

Financial support and dedicated time for the redesign were crucial in bringing partners together. Financial resources, particularly in the form of UPPI grant funding, supported travel for geographically distant partners and allowed organizations to hire individuals to work on UPPI or provide release time for existing staff. Indeed, the UPPI grant funding allowed many organizations to provide individuals with the time to focus on leadership development in a way that such individuals would otherwise not have been able to. Without these resources, the universities would not have been able to build, formalize, and strengthen relationships with their partners, particularly district partners, a necessary ingredient in UPPI.

Cross-site professional learning community meetings also supported partnership engagement. At these multiday meetings convened by The Wallace Foundation and facilitated by the American Institutes for Research, all UPPI teams were invited to learn from other teams engaging in the same redesign work. These professional learning communities also provided all partnerships with access to expertise in the field of school leadership development. Various interviewees reported being motivated and invigorated as an individual and as a team by the professional learning community meetings. Hearing about other partnerships' redesign and learning from experts renewed their commitment to the work and helped the UPPI team engage in deeper thinking about their redesign. For example, some ULs talked about adopting some of the processes and concepts used by other teams (e.g., holding community meetings, sharing out with similar programs and districts). One respondent described hearing about courses that other universities included in their curricula and incorporating one or more of them in some way into their own program's curriculum redesign. One partnership that typically held its UPPI leadership team meetings by phone found in-person professional learning community meetings especially helpful for accomplishing its work.

Challenges and Mitigating Strategies

Several common challenges related to managing the redesign process emerged: issues related to managing time, inefficiencies in managing logistics and other operational aspects of the initiative, institutional bureaucracy, tentative faculty engagement, and the perception of the slow pace of the redesign progress. The challenges were not unsurmountable, and most partnerships have devised strategies to address these issues.

Competing priorities made time management a challenge. ULs struggled to find times when everyone could meet, which involved building in time for travel and dealing with differing university and district calendars (including summer break). Some respondents described setting meetings in advance or offering virtual rather than in-person meetings as ways to overcome this challenge. Respondents also consistently indicated that having time to participate in the redesign on top of their regular workload was very difficult. This challenge was exacerbated in most cases by an insufficient number of personnel (because of staff vacancies or small staff) for UPPI work.

Competing priorities for faculty, such as publishing and getting tenure, often made finding time to engage in UPPI work challenging. District staff also had competing priorities because they did not receive release time for UPPI work. State leads faced similar challenges of not having extra time in their regular workload to take on UPPI-related meetings and work, although state leads were less explicit about this constraint. One state lead described:

> I feel like the work continues to grow, sometimes almost exponentially. Unfortunately for all of us, our other work did not go away and so there's just a lot to pull together, and I guess sometimes it feels like we're getting more and more added onto it, but I don't think that diminishes our positive belief about what we're doing.

Inefficiencies in managing communications and technology hindered early progress. Early in the initiative, there were inefficiencies with respect to managing logistics, communication, technology, and collaboration, all of which initially hindered the work for most partnerships. Project leads perceived these inefficiencies as common startup challenges. Respondents of most partnerships said they struggled to establish protocols for communication, such as how often to communicate or through what mechanism (e.g., email, texting, online platforms). These issues resulted in communica-

Box 4.6

Western Kentucky University and the Green River Regional Educational Cooperative Created a Shared Liaison Position to Smooth Communication and Coordination

WKU and its consortium partner, the Green River Regional Educational Cooperative (GRREC), recognized early on that there was delayed or unclear communication and inefficient coordination between them. To solve the issue, they arranged for a GRREC employee—who had familiarity with key project members from WKU—to be shared with WKU. She would serve as the liaison and project coordinator between the partner organizations. The position was part-time. Funding from WKU for the position came from university dollars; GRREC contributed part of the liaison's salary with UPPI grant funds.

On average, the liaison worked on the WKU campus once or twice a week. She attended calls between WKU and GRREC, as well as some calls that included other partners, and followed up on action items for WKU and GRREC as needed. Among other responsibilities, the liaison kept a budget of the UPPI project for GRREC and an up-to-date budget for WKU. She took care of operational and logistical concerns for both WKU and GRREC project teams, such as securing a room for meetings and posting documents and meeting notes online. The liaison did not engage substantively with the redesign work itself; rather, she worked behind the scenes to ensure that the operational pieces were in place for the work to happen and progress.

tion silos, which hindered the ability to convey messages across all partners (e.g., neglecting to relay redesign decisions across committees or partners, deterring collaboration on tasks). An additional communication issue cited by respondents of some partnerships was that not every partner necessarily had the same working definition for concepts, such as "competency-based instruction." These teams spent time getting all partners to agree on common definitions.

Identifying technology solutions that worked for all partners also was an issue early in the initiative. Some leads realized they had different institutional firewalls and/or network securities that prohibited certain platforms. Over time, teams selected platforms for sharing work and figured out where to store and find documents.

By the end of the first year, most UPPI leadership teams had hired a project coordinator or manager, who helped centralize communication and troubleshoot technological issues. This person liaised between the UL and other project leads and was often responsible for uploading documents onto shared platforms and distributing agendas for meetings, among other managerial tasks. Some teams also leaned on graduate students to ease administrative burdens, while others hired more-senior university personnel to take over aspects of the redesign, thus freeing the UL to focus on key tasks and overall management.

Getting the right people involved in specific aspects of the redesign was initially a challenge. Most partnerships faced issues in filling a specific position for UPPI-related work (e.g., finding an LTS project manager) and determining who should be responsible for certain tasks or serve on certain committees. Respondents said that making sure the right individuals are at the table is essential to the success of UPPI. Such individuals need to be able to make decisions for their organization, have the necessary knowledge for the task, be passionate about making the redesign happen, and be willing to innovate and learn. Being well-connected could also be an asset. One team deliberately hired someone who was well known in the community and had existing relationships with superintendents; this contributed to more successful communication with district leads.

Institutional bureaucracy slowed the change process. Respondents consistently cited institutional bureaucracy, most commonly at the university level, as a challenge. For example, the university process for approving course or curriculum changes is cumbersome; redesigned curricula must go through multiple committees, faculty senates, counsels, boards, and senior university leadership. This process could be incredibly time-consuming and could slow UPPI work. Relatedly, opaque university processes or guidelines were identified as a challenge by some partnerships. For one team, it was unclear to them whether their efforts constituted an entire program change or simply revisions of multiple courses. The former would require substantially more time and effort to complete and process, which would have had significant implications for the redesign work.

> **Box 4.7**
> **A Deputy University-Based Lead Has Been Helpful to North Carolina State University**
>
> NC State decided to bring on a deputy UL to share the UPPI initiative responsibilities. Gradually, the UL worked toward transferring responsibility to her deputy in order to develop capacity within the department. The UL's deputy is a junior faculty member who has less experience managing grants of this size. From the UL's perspective, this opportunity will provide this faculty member with a valuable professional development opportunity and position the individual to take on work of this nature in the future.
>
> The UPPI team moved the work forward by working through an issue together (e.g., content that the curriculum should cover), then the UL and deputy UL took that input and created a product (e.g., a course sequence). Subsequently, the district partners and other UPPI team members reviewed the product and signed off. Ultimately, though, the UL understood her role was to make the final decisions on the redesign.

University funding and staffing policies also have slowed down the change process. Some partnerships had vacant university and district positions because of delays in starting the UPPI contract. University hiring procedures were also time-consuming, especially when hiring district employees for adjunct roles. Finally, funneling the grant money to the districts from the university was complex in some cases.

Teams tried different ways to overcome these bureaucratic challenges. Some planned ahead with the university calendar to ensure that they can meet all course approval and staffing deadlines, some initiated conversations with university senior leaders to get buy-in and help navigate various university policies and guidelines. With respect to the laborious course approval process, ULs identified creative solutions. Some teams made program changes strategically to skirt or postpone official university processes. For example, one team made revisions that did not require changing the course names and numbers; only courses where the names and numbers change are required to go through the university course approval process. Eventually, the program will have to go through the approval process as more substantial curriculum redesign occurs, but this initial strategy saved time early in the redesign. Similarly, another team chose to pilot changes to the courses, which delays the university course change approval process for a few years. ULs also initiated conversations in advance with their dean and relevant departments and offices to identify the most efficient way to navigate the program approval process.

Perception of the slow pace of the redesign progress hindered stakeholder interest. The perceived slow pace of progress made it difficult to sustain the motivation and interest of various stakeholders not directly involved in the day-to-day work of the program redesign. In particular, some district leads were concerned that their superintendents and boards of education might be losing interest in the work because they had little progress to report (on the LTS in particular). For example, one district project lead said:

> You really have to keep people [in the district] motivated and pumped up and excited about the work and let them know that work is still happening, still going on. It may appear that we are at a standstill, but we are still making progress. That's the main thing.

One district lead perceived the LTS "was not exciting" to the superintendent and other cabinet members yet because they had not yet actually seen it. Finally, leads from another district articulated:

> While we are all about learning, there is a need for efficiency and execution. We live in an environment where things need to get done tomorrow. . . . We need to execute because given where we are fiscally as well as in terms of academic performance with our students, there is a sense of urgency to get something done. We don't . . . have the luxury of slowing down.

To try to hold stakeholder attention, leads continued to provide regular progress updates and, when possible, made connections to work that was of interest to stakeholders. For example, one district lead reported that the superintendent and members of the cabinet perked up and started to discuss the LTS when he linked the LTS to the system the district was trying to develop for tracking teachers and open teaching positions.

Leadership turnover disrupted the momentum of the work and partner engagement. Teams experienced turnover in multiple key positions, including the UPPI project manager, university faculty, university administration, district superintendents, and state partner leads throughout the first year of the redesign. Changing partners was challenging, particularly for the university programs because it required them to onboard the new person, get them up to speed with the work to date, and build new trusting working relationships. As one UL said:

> Partnerships are institutional, [and] they're very much built on relationships. And when you invest all your effort into building these relationships and the training, and then to have that person move on, and then have to start all over again, it is frustrating.

From another perspective, incoming members felt the challenge as well. Newcomers needed time to learn about all the nuances of the initiative and about their roles in the partnership. As one district superintendent said:

> I think maybe right at the beginning, for me it was [challenging]. The former superintendent had worked with [the university] on the grant and what that was going to look like. And I came in after those conversations had already occurred. And so, it was kind of like I was trying to figure out what is our role and what is it going to look like [in our district].

> **Box 4.8**
> **Strategies for Mitigating the Effects of UPPI Partnership Member Turnover**
> - **Clear goals, timelines, and documentation of the work** allowed teams to maintain focus when members left and new members joined. When established collaboratively as a team, these goals and timelines have helped to ensure buy-in and agreement.
> - **ULs met individually with new team members** to orient the individual to the initiative and review the logic models, goals, and timelines. Any additional documentation helped the new team member get up to speed on the initiative.
> - **Cross-training team members** in the UPPI work helped ensure that there were shared knowledge, roles, and responsibilities. This helped reduce the loss of institutional knowledge when a key member left the UPPI team.

A related challenge was that, for some partnerships, new leadership brought in new priorities that might not align with UPPI. One UL described the challenge as follows:

> I'm concerned about [the partner district] . . . because of the fact they have a new superintendent. . . . [The] outstanding question is whether or not he makes UPPI a priority. Based on what I'm hearing because of all of the challenges they currently have in their school system, UPPI is not a priority.

Over time, teams developed and used several strategies to help mitigate the disruption in work resulting from turnover. With clear goals, timelines, and documentation of what has been achieved thus far, most UPPI partners were able to maintain focus on the work. Some teams used their program redesign logic models to brief new members on the initiative. ULs said they intentionally reached out to new staff members and leaders within the university and across partner organizations to update them on the initiative and invite them to meetings. One UL described this process: "I spent a lot of hours in [the new district UPPI program coordinator's] office. . . . I met with her and basically showed her what we were doing and helped her to envision what she wanted to do." Another, more preemptive strategy was to cross-train team members on different roles and tasks so that in case of turnover, knowledge about the initiative would not be not lost; another capable individual would be prepared to step in and fill the role.

Summary

The program redesign required individuals from distinctly different organizations with varying skill sets, time commitments, and management philosophies to determine the best ways to work together toward a common goal. Although UPPI teams have approached the management process in different ways, they have all adopted some common approaches, such as establishing regular communication methods and procedures, delegating of responsibilities and workloads, and building a positive culture of trust and continuous improvement. The ULs have played a pivotal role in keeping teams moving forward on UPPI's many complex and competing tasks and have been champions for change. The first year of UPPI may have been the most challenging for the management of the redesign, because the partnerships have had to work to establish shared tools and procedures. All teams have mitigated the challenges they faced by staying focused on the goals of the UPPI initiative.

CHAPTER FIVE

Changing the Context for School Leader Preparation

Research has found that effective principal preparation programs operate in supportive contexts marked by partnerships between university programs and the school districts they serve; a state context that uses standards to drive program improvement through accreditation and school leader certification, as well as support for current and aspiring administrators; and financial support for program participants. In addition to promoting change within university programs themselves, UPPI expected teams to look outward and work in partnership with district, state, and other collaborators to change key elements of the context for school leader preparation. Indeed, within just the first year, the redesign initiative has motivated changes in policy and practice across multiple sites. The initiative put special emphasis on one context element that spans the university program and state and district partners: leader tracking systems to support program improvement. This emphasis was reflected in targeted support and expectations for developing LTSs.

In this chapter, we identify and discuss changes in the state and district contexts linked to the UPPI effort, including findings from the development of LTSs within the districts.

State Context

Research suggests that exemplary principal preparation programs benefit from a supportive state policy context. UPPI provided funding to the state entity responsible for accrediting principal preparation programs, with the expectation that the state entity would review state policies related to principal preparation programs, including but not limited to accreditation. The state partners were expected to engage with other state entities and stakeholder groups to strengthen the state's policy environment related to school leader preparation. Additionally, state partners attended meetings at The Wallace Foundation, where they were able to interact with officials from other states on UPPI and ESSA issues.

UPPI state partners were either state departments of education or professional standards or credentialing commissions. Some state-level organizations that were not part of the initial team later joined to support the implementation of UPPI. State departments of education are often responsible for introducing new rules and regulations around principal preparation, regulations that could support or hinder UPPI and similar future efforts. State departments of education are also responsible for developing the ESSA state plans, which can include plans for improving the quality of school leadership. These plans provide an opportunity for the states to ensure that UPPI priorities are aligned with long-term state priorities. While some states did ensure this alignment, at least one of the seven states did not. In this case, the state department of education was aware of UPPI and supported the initiative, but it was not an official partner. As such, the UPPI team felt there was a missed opportunity to have leadership be a bigger focus of the state's ESSA plan; however, the UPPI team was not able to influence the ESSA plan.

State professional organizations (e.g., principals' or administrators' associations) also engaged by providing access to communication mechanisms that reach administrators statewide. Professional organizations can also be influential in state policymaking by having representation on state-level education policy committees or connections to key state policymakers. Their involvement could secure support from their constituencies and provide resources to help sustain the work accomplished as part of UPPI. In one state, for example, the state association of education leadership professors is helping create state-level policy task forces around educational leadership that would align with UPPI redesign efforts.

As described by Manna (2015), the state context influences principal preparation programs in a number of ways. The most direct lever is through their authority to approve and oversee principal preparation programs. States can leverage this authority by establishing requirements for approved programs that, in turn, can promote program change. For example, as the UPPI was launching, one state was in the process of developing and piloting a new performance-based examination. Passing this examination would eventually be required of all individuals completing a state-approved administrative credential program. Both the state and the UPPI leadership teams viewed this new requirement as a driver for changes to both curriculum and clinical experiences. A less direct but still important lever for influencing program content is through credentialing new and current administrators. By establishing expectations about the knowledge, skills, and abilities that school administrators must demonstrate, states can indirectly influence program content and structure. Candidates who want to be prepared for the state credentialing process will seek out programs that are aligned with those requirements.

State partner engagement in UPPI led to some concrete policy reforms. Some states have adopted new or revised state-level leader standards. According to interviewees, this was a direct result of their participation in the initiative. For example, one state standards commission recognized the need to change its state leader standards based on the analysis work conducted through UPPI, which highlighted gaps between the state's standards and the national PSEL standards. This state then approved the adoption of new PSEL state standards on an accelerated timeline so the university could avoid having to work with old state standards.

Some states have adopted or considered rule or process changes because of their participation in UPPI. For example, one state explored the possibility of requiring all programs seeking accreditation to engage in a formative assessment, akin to QM, midway through their program approval cycle. As the state lead said, "I would like to see [QM] become part of our program approval process. . . . It is a fabulous formative measure that could be used maybe three years into program approval as an interim measure that would help us and the institution see if they are still on track. . . . We would not be pursuing that if it were not for UPPI." In another instance, the state sought to motivate program change across the state from the ground up by offering programs the opportunity to engage in a formative exercise such as QM free of cost.

Other states worked on redefining or clarifying the purpose and requirements of Level 1 and Level 2 educational leadership certification programs, which had been problematic for the UPPI program in those states. That is, some states have two (or more) levels, or tiers, of certification for school administrators. In some cases (e.g., California, Connecticut), candidates with tier 1 certification can assume a principalship. To stay in the position, they are required to achieve tier 2 certification by completing additional courses and satisfactory experience. In other states (e.g., Florida, Georgia), level 1 certification holders are typically eligible for assistant principalship; candidates need to complete a level 2 programs to be eligible for level 2 certification and principalship.

UPPI stimulated other state initiatives related to educational leadership. Some state partners have added a focus on educational leadership to the agenda for regular gatherings of state-level organizations. Key aspects of the redesign work, including QM and logic models, have also been integrated in statewide summits. For example, UPPI programs shared their positive feedback on the QM process at state-level meetings in two states; other programs expressed interest in doing something similar. This prompted the state departments of education in these two states to make the self-assessment process available to other programs. In another example, the work under UPPI informed the development and implementation of new state assessments for administrative candidates in some states.

UPPI encouraged some states to consider scaling elements of UPPI throughout the state. Most partners also saw the potential of UPPI and have articulated a vision to scale pieces of the UPPI work throughout the state. In one case, the state partner wanted to replicate the university-district partnership framework and the feedback loops that those partnerships support. Some state partners have used the UPPI-supported statewide gatherings to convey learning from UPPI to all university-based principal preparation programs in the state. In helping to communicate about the UPPI work and encourage sharing of best practices across the state, the state partners laid the groundwork for potentially scaling up the program redesign efforts. For example, at one statewide meeting, the university program reported on key program changes resulting from UPPI; the state shared policy updates; then the principal preparation programs in attendance were given time to collaborate and share best practices.

State partners provided strategic advice on program redesign. Some state leads participated in UPPI leadership team meetings, offering input and suggestions about the program redesign. State leads used their knowledge as policymakers and regulators to help the UPPI team navigate state regulations and meet state standards around principal preparation. This input was especially useful in states where the state partner organization would have to approve the redesigned programs. As described by one UL:

> The state . . . has been engaged with us because ultimately we need to submit the redesigned program to [them]. . . . It's been helpful having [the state] there to stay on track. In addition to the national standards, we understand the politics of the state too because of [the state lead's involvement].

Likewise, one district lead recognized this support from the state partner:

> That's also the blessing of having the state department right there . . . at the table [to be able to] talk about standards and requirements have been instrumental.

Another UL described the state's willingness to facilitate and navigate the political climate to move the UPPI work forward:

> [The state partner] is poised, and [it is] ready to do what [it needs] to do, but it's just good to know that [it] really understands the importance of this, and [it is] willing to have conversations. [It is] willing to use whatever political [leverage] that [it] may have in order to facilitate our ability to do what we need to do with the least amount of resistance.

However, not all states were able to serve in the role because of concerns about appearing to favor one program in the state over others.

Finally, some state leads helped districts with their LTS development efforts, making sure the districts' LTSs leverage and align with the state data systems and providing guidance on data sharing and privacy concerns.

Contextual issues unrelated to UPPI posed challenges for state engagement in UPPI. Despite their willingness to be involved, some states faced financial constraints that limited the availability and capacity of state partner leads to attend regular UPPI meetings and other special gatherings. These states reported being short-staffed; as a result, their employees often took on multiple roles and had to juggle competing priorities. One district lead described its state partner's challenges: "The state has been one of the last groups to come to the table. I just think that [it's] busy and [its] budget's been cut and [it's] knee deep in all kinds of other turmoil."

Political issues also challenged state engagement. New state administrations or the anticipation of new administrations hampered one state's ability to prioritize and fully dedicate time and resources to UPPI. The staff members at this state's partner organization had little to no direction about their roles in the organization, so they were hesitant to become more involved in UPPI than attending meetings and staying current with the initiative. One university UL described a precarious situation:

> With our new [state] superintendent, there's just been a lot of [distractions]. So, there's no vision right now, there's no sense of direction. The State Department of Education is worried, everyone's worried they're going to be downsized or fired. . . . So it's hard to get a sense of where are we moving.

On the other hand, in some states facing fiscal challenges, state partners looked to UPPI as an opportunity to engage in state-level work that had been defunded. For example, one state with a budget shortfall and staff shortages had a vision to transform both teacher preparation and leader preparation. While the teacher preparation task force completed its work, the state-level leader preparation committee was terminated. The state partner explained, "We have the opportunity now through UPPI to do what we would have done. And so, we feel like this is our opportunity to get at transforming principal prep."

District Context

Research indicates that exemplary principal preparation programs are facilitated by a supportive context in partner districts. An explicit expectation for districts participating in the UPPI is that they would provide the programs with data on the performance of program graduates to support continuous improvement on the part of the preparation program. To meet this expectation, districts were asked and provided with support to develop an LTS on their own or in collaboration with other districts. UPPI partners—especially districts, which have primary responsibility for the LTS—were encouraged to think of additional ways in which the LTS would be useful.

Some district partners have identified a need for changes to principal hiring practices as a result of their participation in UPPI. Specifically, participants of one UPPI partnership attributed their decision to change their program screening and hiring processes to the influence of their mentor program and other exemplar district leadership programs that they had access to through UPPI. Meanwhile, another district developed new hiring processes that are more systematic and that generate more data to inform continuous program improvement (e.g., by adopting rubrics). In this case, the idea emerged through informal conversations with other district partners and the university program. Still another district partner began creating new rubrics to support its hiring processes that were now aligned to the university's program standards.

District partners were also inspired by UPPI to revisit their principal evaluation criteria. Some district partners began implementing revisions to their existing administrator evaluation tools and creating new evaluation tools where none existed (in both cases, aligned to the university's program standards). Other districts considered revising their administrator job descriptions based on the UPPI work to align them to the new program-level leader standards and associated performance expectations.

UPPI partnership has enhanced collaboration on matters outside the program redesign. For example, building on UPPI connections, one university-district partnership began collaborating on an initiative to improve the diversity of the teaching work force. In addition, some UPPI partner organizations have begun working together on new initiatives related to teacher recruitment and preparation. Some district partners of one university program, for example, have expressed interest in working with the university to develop a pathway to teaching for paraprofessionals. One other university saw a possibility of expanding the scope of its principal preparation program to include principal induction activities, which are currently managed exclusively by district partners.

District leads also reported collaborating more with other district leads as a result of their common engagement in UPPI. For example, within some teams, district partner leads reported sharing best practices on leadership development and recruitment as well as tools and resources, such as hiring rubrics and principal evaluation protocols. According to one district lead, "We're reaching out to each other with just questions about our job and about the [human resources] kind of functions that we run into." Another district partner described other district leads as "thought partners" on topics related to and outside of UPPI. Still another district director described the emerging inter-district collaboration as a "community of practice."

UPPI has expanded professional learning opportunities for current and aspiring administrators in some partner districts. For some partners, participation in UPPI has provided access to new professional learning opportunities across and outside the district partners. For example, district partners have been invited to professional development activities organized by the mentor program or by the other district partners. UPPI has also prompted new intra-district initiatives. For example, districts across most of the partnerships have begun either revising their existing professional development activities for administrators and administrative candidates or considering developing or beginning to develop their own in-house leadership academies and programs. These academies are broadly intended to support districts' efforts to "grow their own leaders." In some cases, district partners targeted teacher leaders; in other cases, such emerging efforts focused on professional development for new assistant principals, experienced assistant principals who desire to move into the principalship, new principals, or other sitting administrators. One university considered building an assistant principal academy.

Additional districts engaged in UPPI informally. One university recruited an additional neighboring district to help address capacity issues at its smallest district. The UL explained how this helped:

> I basically use [an additional district] to fill in where [the partner district] can't. For example, in the course work groups, there are holes. . . . . [The partner district] couldn't find Ph.D.-holding administrators to do some of the work, so I pulled in people from [an additional district].

The UL of another partnership also reached out and engaged a few larger neighboring districts unofficially in UPPI. These districts served a similar population of students as the UPPI partner districts, and it was likely that some of the graduates from the redesigned program would ultimately be placed in these newly engaged districts, given their size and need.

District Leader Tracking System Efforts

Prior to UPPI, the participating university programs—like most preparation programs—lacked systematic approaches to tracking the progress of their graduates. All seven partnerships have dedicated significant time and effort in the first year to establishing the structures that need to be in place and identifying the types of data that the LTS will warehouse. Partners, especially district partners, have identified relevant data sources typically housed in different offices across the district, university program, and state. The partners have also identified existing structures and structures that will need to be developed to support the data system. In 2018, the districts will select a vendor and begin the work of developing the system.

As required by UPPI, all partner districts worked to develop an LTS to inform program improvement, in some cases in close collaboration with the state. The UPPI included explicit expectations and funding support for developing data systems to support the col-

> **Box 5.1**
> **Leader Tracking Systems**
>
> An LTS is "a database with longitudinal information about current and aspiring principals that would potentially support data-driven decisionmaking regarding principal selection, hiring, and support" (Kaufman et al., 2017). In UPPI, districts are to lead the development of such a system, which would interface with the data system at the university in order to provide the preparation program with data on program graduates' performance, including placement rates. Developing an LTS requires districts "to identify all the relevant data sources regarding current and aspiring principals (typically housed in different district offices across the district); address issues with data quality, including critical gaps in the data; compile the data into a usable, longitudinal format; and develop user-friendly systems through which district personnel could access information that would meet their most-pressing needs" (Kaufman et al., 2017; for more on LTS, also see Anderson et al., 2017; Gill, 2016).

lection and sharing of information about program participants between programs and districts. These data systems would provide university programs with critical information not currently available about the outcomes of program graduates, such as whether they have obtained an administrative position, their performance in such a position, and whether they have attained or achieved desired leadership competencies. The programs, in turn, would be able to use this information for continuous improvement. The initiative gave teams a fair amount of flexibility with respect to designing and structuring the LTS, although the presumption was that district partners would lead the effort.

University and district partners see different uses for LTS data. In their work plans for the first year of UPPI, the partnerships committed to developing an LTS, and almost all teams indicated that the LTS would serve two purposes: "Develop and implement [an LTS] to meet the needs of the district and . . . provide data to the university on the job performance of its graduates." For the most part, the university program seek data from an LTS to inform continuous program improvement. This involves accessing data and feedback on their graduates to understand graduate outcomes, such as when they undertake their first principalship position and their effectiveness in that role. Given such information, program could potentially target improvements in specific aspects of their programs, including their candidate recruitment and selection criteria and procedures, curriculum content coverage, instructional approach, and the extent and types of required clinical experiences. One university administrator said:

> We are very excited about the tracking system. This is one of the levels of frustration that we have right now. Our graduates leave, and they just are kind of swallowed up by the district, and we don't know where they are or how they're doing.

Meanwhile, district partners planned to use the LTS to inform their own operations. They envisioned the LTS as a centralized source from which they could pull information on demographic characteristics, educational background, certification, job placements, job performance, school and student-level performance, competencies, and dispositions for aspiring and current principals to better understand their strengths and weaknesses. That information would help them identify potential leaders within their organization and to place, manage, and further develop program graduates and active principals.

While the two sets of expectations—those of the university program and those of district partners—are not mutually exclusive, having different sets of data needs and access may present some challenges. To fulfill both purposes, the system would need to hold a sizable amount of data—feedback on program graduates and information on aspiring principals—and draw from different existing databases. Further, data protections become an issue when some of the LTS information need to be communicated outside the district, to the university program.

Two organizational models for the LTS emerged. Two primary LTS organizational models emerged: (1) a single LTS across partner districts and (2) a district-specific LTS. The single LTS model will have one data system that all district, university, and potentially state data feed into (Figure 5.1). It appears that for partnerships where a regional consortium is involved, the preferred model of LTS under consideration is a more centralized system. Partnerships with this model saw the possibility of expanding their LTS to a statewide LTS, to which both partner districts and other districts in the state would contribute and have access. Meanwhile, district-specific LTS will have separate data systems for each partner district. In this model, most district-specific LTS will share common data elements, such as statewide longitudinal data, but each district-specific LTS will also include data that relate to each district's unique needs. Factors such as differences in district size, current data capabilities, and existing relationships with other districts played a role in deciding on the LTS model. It is not yet clear whether the resulting LTSs will meet both the university program and district needs effectively. The systems are slated to be developed and piloted in 2018.

The first stage of the LTS effort involved developing an overall vision statement, warehousing data, and planning for the development of the RFP. UPPI teams went through an intensive process to create an LTS vision statement. The partnerships established the knowledge, competencies, and dispositions that define an effective school leader in order to inform the type of data they desired to track. To do so, the teams drew on past experiences and professional standards (national, state, and local district standards). Simultaneously, they identified available data sources and elements that were already being collected to ensure that they would not reinvent the wheel and to locate where they can potentially pull existing data elements. Most teams are still in the process of developing and releasing an RFP to secure a vendor to develop

Figure 5.1
Two Primary Models of Leader Tracking Systems

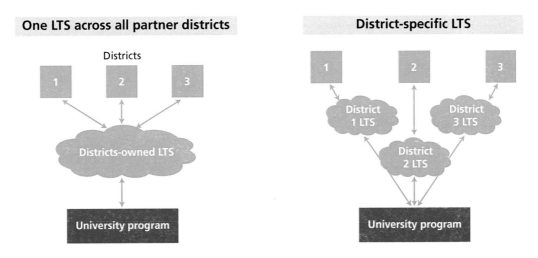

the system. They are involving their technology staffs in developing the RFPs. One partnership has already issued an RFP and selected a vendor.

Exposure to existing and model LTS was helpful. In the beginning, all partnerships struggled with the abstractness of LTS—what it would look like and how it would work—until they saw operating examples of existing LTSs. For example, ULs and district leads visited other districts or participated in webinars to view existing LTS models. A district lead described a live webinar with representatives from Gwinnett County Public Schools's Quality Plus Leader Academy and Hillsborough Public Schools[1] as being particularly valuable because it provided an opportunity "to listen to those two districts and to have them discuss their successes, their best practices, and how the LTS supports their districts." District-specific LTS demonstrations gave teams an opportunity to see how the LTS interacts with districts and university programs. Some teams also visited universities that had created similar data systems. Seeing a model LTS helped university program and district leads envision the type of data they could collect and the type of problems and questions they could use the LTS to solve.

Partnerships saw potential challenges related to data accessibility and LTS functionality. First, if the LTS will house or pull data about candidates from campus student records systems, issues around the Family Educational Rights and Privacy Act (FERPA) may need to be navigated; there needs to be assurance that entities that should not have access to such records (e.g., districts, states) in fact do not. A second issue is that, because LTS data will derive from multiple sources, partner leads expressed concern about inconsistency in data collection and data restrictions. For example, for one partnership, principal evaluation data were not collected across all district partners, and another district had a union that placed limits on the use of principal data. This scenario poses potential challenges when the UPPI leadership team wants to obtain the same information across all district partners. Also, given the amount and breadth of data available within an LTS, some partnerships worried that the system may be overwhelming to use. There is the risk of the LTS sitting idle if little explicit attention is paid to ensuring its usability.

Strategies to mitigate these challenges included actively thinking about the LTS interface and communication across data systems early on, seeing how model LTSs have navigated this process, and involving internal information technology personnel. Specifically with respect to information security and data privacy, all UPPI teams recognized the LTS must address these issues in a way that complies with federal, state, and local policies. They recognized, for example, that some districts are unionized and some are not, which has implications for how data can be shared and accessed. Having state partners, and sometimes union representation, as part of the partnership has helped to provide clarity on legal issues associated with data sharing and collection.

---

[1]   These districts were funded by The Wallace Foundation's Principal Pipeline initiative.

Summary

UPPI has prompted the organizations involved to consider issues and/or undertake activities they may not have otherwise, with implications for the context in which the university program operates.

Engaging in the program redesign process has led some states to consider—and even carry out—policy and practice changes, such as revising state-level leader standards, including leadership in state events, and considering scaling QM statewide. State partners also engaged with the teams to help carry out the redesign work, especially in providing guidance on how to align that work with state requirements. However, limitations in staff time and political sensitivities were challenges to state engagement.

Similarly, through their participation in the redesign work, some districts have begun to reassess policies, such as district hiring practices, and to work more closely across districts. Partly by design, the preparation program work has begun to extend into professional development for sitting principals. And districts have begun to plan and build the LTS that will help them systematically track and use data about potential and sitting principals.

CHAPTER SIX

Key Insights

For this final chapter, we step back from discussing discrete findings about each of the research questions—about progress with respect to program redesign, management of the change process, and partner engagement—to survey the key insights we have identified across various topics. In doing so, we draw out some overarching emerging conclusions about the first year of UPPI implementation. First, we identify some main drivers of the initiative. Then, we synthesize the major challenges and mitigating strategies from the various chapters. Next, we discuss some lessons learned. Finally, we offer a summary of emerging conclusions.

Main Drivers of UPPI

In considering the various factors respondents identified as facilitators of the program redesign, management of the redesign process, and partner engagement, four main drivers emerged. Some of these drivers appeared to keep the work on track or even propel it forward, while some helped to navigate challenges encountered.

ULs keep UPPI on track. According to multiple respondents across all programs, the ULs may be the most important driver of the redesign work. At the beginning of the initiative in particular, they were instrumental in strategically identifying partner organizations and individuals to participate. They reportedly used their influence and relationships to ensure that the right people were engaged in the initiative. Furthermore, they worked to develop and secure buy-in from top-level organization leaders both at the beginning of UPPI and as turnover occurred. In addition to being critical for partnership-building and partner engagement, ULs have exhibited commendable organization, management, and problem-solving skills—all necessary for a smooth change process. They communicated extensively and continuously about UPPI internally within the university program, with university administrators, with the UPPI partners, and beyond, with external stakeholders. All the while, ULs were sensitive to the unique contexts of their partners and region; they identified meaningful and mutually beneficial ways for various partners to engage in the program redesign, while accounting for the capacity limitations of each organization. Because of their skills, commitment, and enthusiasm, the ULs are viewed as a main driver of the initiative.

Collaboration, engagement, and passion on the part of partners drove the work forward. Even an effective UL would not likely be able to steer as complex and ambitious an initiative as UPPI alone. Multiple respondents from various UPPI teams recognized that partner organizations' and individuals' motivation and willingness to do what it takes to achieve the common vision helped to keep the work moving forward. As one interviewee described it,

> There's a lot of passion. . . . Everyone is committed to making sure this [redesign] is successful. That's so evident. We so much want this to be successful. We have a sense of urgency and passion. I think it's coming from the perspective that we want this to be very, very successful that we do what we feel is necessary to get the job done.

Indeed, selected partners appeared to have very willingly engaged in the initiative, driven by visions of better prepared school leaders who are ready to step into the role on day one. District leads regarded whatever effort was required for UPPI as worthwhile, given the anticipated dividends for their schools, students, and communities in the years to come. It was in the districts' interest to partner with a university willing to engage in continuous improvement, because the districts' candidates—and program's graduates—would have great potential to lead effective schools and affect student achievement and growth. State partners also exhibited commitment toward UPPI and its focus on leadership reform. They looked to UPPI as a test bed for innovative and rigorous leader preparation reform ideas that are anchored in evidence-based practices. They looked to the UPPI as a potential model to use in supporting other higher education institutions in the state to improve their programs. Despite the amount of time and energy involved, partner organizations and individuals engaged in the initiative with purpose, and this was critical in keeping the work on track.

Resources, in the form of time and professional learning opportunities, helped deepen engagement and elevate the work. UPPI teams learned that transformative program redesign required time and space to be intentional in their process and thoughtful in their decisionmaking. Financial support in the form of the UPPI grant was instrumental, because it allowed many organizations—universities and districts alike—to provide select individuals with release time from their regular responsibilities to engage fully in UPPI. Otherwise, the costs may have been prohibitive for districts to engage as deeply as they would have liked; partnerships and the flow of the work may have suffered.

While travel to professional learning community meetings was a burden for many individuals—because of the travel itself and time spent away from their regular position—multiple participants agreed that such meetings were invaluable. For some, they provided (extra) opportunities for UPPI leadership teams to meet and work together face-to-face, and in so doing they bolstered partnership building and engagement. Professional learning communities also enabled partnerships to elevate their work through cross-pollination of ideas with the other UPPI teams and additional available expertise. Being involved in an improvement network, as it were, kept the partnerships on track in terms of both engagement and the rigor and substance of the redesign.

The logic model development process and the logic model itself served multiple purposes that advanced the redesign. The logic model development process supported various facets of UPPI implementation. Working toward this deliverable early on encouraged partners to agree on a vision and to develop strategies to accomplish the end goal. Through this process, partners had the opportunity to understand each other's perspectives and challenges. In this way, the logic model exercise helped to build partnerships and generate commitment to, and motivation for, the work.

Partnerships used logic models in various ways. They found that the models supported communication within the team and could be used to message the work of the team to incoming members and to external stakeholders. Logic models, along with timelines and work statements, also served to keep the team focused on the goals, particularly when competing priorities threatened their progress.

Common Challenges and Mitigating Strategies

Synthesizing across the challenges described in various chapters, we identified two major categories of challenges that hampered UPPI implementation and redesign progress: contextual challenges and challenges related to individual capacity.

A range of institutional or contextual challenges threatened UPPI implementation. The most commonly reported challenge was turnover in leadership roles in UPPI or in a partner organization, which threatened the continuity of support and vision. Partnerships experiencing turnover often had to pause the work to onboard a new member. Leadership turnover also jeopardized engagement across the team; participants reported feeling uncertain as to whether new leaders would embrace the initiative or disregard it as a priority. Multiple turnovers at one time or within one organization could lead to the perception that the initiative was unstable or unsustainable; at a minimum, it placed additional onus on the original and remaining members to carry and share the vision.

Another type of contextual challenge involved institutional guidelines, mainly within the university. Traditional university guidelines challenged innovative approaches to program structure and delivery. Related, traditional—and sometimes opaque—university guidelines complicated the program and curriculum approval process. While UPPI leadership teams aimed to design the best program possible, concern about these guidelines made them wary about having their program redesign stuck in the approval process.

Partnerships relied on ULs to mitigate these challenges and move the work forward. They did so by keeping the team focused on the goal, helping new leaders transition into the UPPI leadership team, and communicating with the university dean and provost about course approval and with state officials about implications of UPPI for policy. Some teams activated more preemptive strategies (e.g., cross-training members for multiple roles in the UPPI leadership team and mapping deadlines for course approval) early on to help guard against contingencies.

Engaging the right individuals with the capacity to be deeply committed was difficult. Personnel capacity was another major challenge. Not finding or bringing the right individuals on board—those with the right skills, passion, time, and the connections and position within one's organization to prioritize this initiative—hindered partner engagement and progress. Even when the right group of individuals was involved, capacity was still an issue. The majority of UPPI participants from all organizations—university, districts, and state—continued in their full-time positions while engaged in UPPI. Competing priorities created a time-management challenge for individuals and for the partnership in terms of finding common times and convenient ways to meet.

Some partnerships found it difficult to engage university faculty. Some faculty members regarded the redesign as too much change too quickly or had concerns that the potential direction of the redesigned program would create unwelcome changes and affect their ownership of the current program. Of course, faculty also had to juggle their existing workloads while engaging in UPPI.

Teams drew on several strategies to mitigate the challenges related to engaging the right people. These included, first, selecting partners with whom they had had a prior relationship, so that buy-in and commitment were already established, and being strategic about who was brought on board. In addition, teams found ways to either provide some release time to individuals or to connect UPPI work with existing initiatives so that their effort could serve both purposes. For faculty, this included making time in department meetings to discuss UPPI redesign.

Lessons Learned

Across partnerships, UPPI participants articulated several lessons learned to date about the UPPI approach. Collectively, these lessons mirror the findings on key drivers and challenges.

Selecting partner organizations and individuals intentionally is crucial. University respondents learned that, from the outset, selecting the right organizations to partner with and the right individuals within each organization to serve in key roles is crucial. On an organizational level, a university administrator defined desirable partner organizations as those that share innovative approaches to preparing leaders. Similarly, district partners expressed the importance of "nimble" faculty who are open to change. Various UPPI participants learned that it is important to have the right individuals on board. Ideally, such individuals should possess excellent communication skills, be a strong voice within their organization, be willing to advocate for activities and decisions within their organization that will help achieve UPPI goals, be able to operationalize redesign ideas, and be willing to see the bigger picture of the initiative even when confronted by obstacles. UPPI participants believed that these types of organizations and individuals will provide the motivation and capacity needed to propel the work forward.

Developing strong relationships early on encourages commitment and supports progress. Respondents from all seven partnerships reported learning the importance of developing strong relationships with partners—both organizationally and individually—early in the initiative. Respondents realized that doing so helps build commitment to the partnership and initiative. In the case of turnover of a UPPI leadership team member, strong organization-level relationships can also mitigate against the loss of partner organization support for the initiative. Beyond the initiative, strong relationships also form the foundation for sustaining improvement efforts beyond the UPPI funding. Taking time to build a strong partnership also helps ensure that the resulting program redesign will fulfill its aims and meet the needs of partners. Strong partners will feel at ease to express their honest opinions about program components and be receptive to critical feedback.

Teams also learned that communication is crucial for sustaining relationships. Multiple institutions stressed the importance of communicating often and openly across organizations. Direct and transparent messaging to all partners helped to establish trust and shared ownership of the redesign process. Moreover, being clear about the roles that each partner is expected to play made them more able and willing to engage and commit to the work. Within one's organization, continuous communication with stakeholders helped with buy-in, which supports mobilization of resources when needed.

There are benefits associated with early uncertainty and a slow process. Unsurprisingly, teams also reported learning that working to effect change requires patience and commitment to a process that may seem painfully slow at times. While some ULs, district leads, and others expressed frustration at the apparent slow pace of progress, they also recognized the benefit of taking the time, especially early on, to build a common understanding of goals, processes, and roles. In most cases, reaching a common understanding helped reduce the confusion and uncertainty often found in a large initiative. Oftentimes, partnerships worked backward from the common goal to determine the processes and roles that would help them achieve their goal. Similarly, some teams recognized that, despite the struggle, it was worth the time investment to create new structures to support change instead of using existing arrangements. For example, partnerships were not exposed to existing LTSs early on in the process, which encouraged them to think outside the box and consider what effective school leadership meant within their own context. Finally, as one district lead expressed:

> Even though you do that scope of work in the beginning and you have every intent to fulfill everything at the time that you had outlined in the scope of work, it just will not happen that way. The work will get done, but it may not get done on the timeline that you had initially planned.

Conclusions from the First Year

UPPI entails a systemic effort on the part of a network of at least four types of organizations (university, school districts or consortium, state agency, and mentor program), each with unique institutional and contextual backgrounds. It requires the partnerships to redesign four program features (curriculum and instruction, clinical experiences, candidate recruitment and selection, and cohort structure), drawing on evidence on effective principal preparation, and to develop an LTS to help inform continuous program improvement. Any number of challenges could have resulted in ineffective blueprints for program redesign, mismanagement of the change process, and partner disengagement.

Thus far, all seven partnerships appear to be standing up to the challenge. Teams dedicated the first year to developing relationships, engaging partners, finding ways to move the work forward, and initiating the program redesign. All teams made progress in curriculum redesign and planning for the LTS. Specifically, by the end of 2017, through benchmarking against national, state, and locally developed professional standards, each UPPI leadership team had identified gaps in its curriculum and developed a course scope and sequence; using the backward-design approach, some teams began rethinking the milestone program assessments and will later consider how to teach the content.

In line with the goal of UPPI, advancements in curriculum redesign moved toward evidence-based best practices for principal development and away from what had been previously identified as deficiencies in typical university principal preparation programs. Drawing on their partners' expertise, UPPI leadership teams are moving toward making their programs more grounded in real-world experiences of school leaders. Working through early uncertainties, most partnerships also arrived at clear visions of an LTS that would both help university programs engage in continuous improvement and support districts to identify, develop, and more effectively place leaders within their system. The Wallace Foundation's funding has been instrumental in supporting the partnerships' work thus far by providing individuals with release time to devote to the work and by supporting professional learning communities to enhance partnership engagement. In all, it appears that the UPPI teams have established a firm foundation of partnerships, articulated a common vision, developed approaches to manage the work, and initiated redesign of multiple program components.

Program and Partners Baseline Descriptions

In this appendix, we provide a brief description of each university's principal preparation program at baseline, that is, before UPPI (see Table A.1). This information will help us track and assess the program changes that have taken place and that are to come in the remaining years of UPPI. We also briefly list the site partners (see Table A.2) and profile each of the district, state, and provider organizations each program has partnered with to engage in the program redesign to acknowledge their role in the initiative and to provide readers with a basic understanding of important contextual conditions.

The information presented here was gathered from publicly available sources. This included websites maintained by each organization as well as U.S. Department of Education databases, such as the National Center for Education Statistics (U.S. Department of Education, 2017a), which reported data from 2015–2016 and 2016–2017, and the Office of Civil Rights' Civil Right Data Collection, which reported data from its 2013 survey (U.S. Department of Education, 2017b). In addition, we drew on information gathered in interviews with the ULs, partner district leads, state partner leads, and mentor program leads.

Table A.1
UPPI Principal Preparation Programs at Baseline (2015–2016)

University	Program Under Redesign	Degree/Endorsement for Certification	State Context	# of Program Credits	# of Students (Regional/District-Based Cohort)	# of Faculty	Clinical Experience Requirement
Albany State University	Educational Leadership	Ed.S. (6th year)/Georgia Professional (Tier II) certification	Tier II programs prepare candidates for advanced leadership positions that include P–12 school-level principals or the equivalent, superintendents, or other local education agency staff who supervise principals (program candidates must be in leadership role—assistant principal or higher)	30–36	34 (0 district-based cohort)	4 + 0 adjuncts	12 credits
Florida Atlantic University	K–12 Educational Leadership	M.Ed./Florida Level 1 certification	Level I programs typically prepares candidates as assistant principals	33	150 (1 district-based cohort)	20 + 15 adjuncts	6 credits
North Carolina State University	Educational Leadership (focus on on-campus track)	MSA/North Carolina School Administrator License	License allows holder to take on either assistant principal or principal positions	24	64 (NELA cohort) 38 (MSA)	12 + 6 adjuncts	18 credits
San Diego State University	PK–12 Educational Leadership	M.A./California Preliminary Administrative Services Credential	Preliminary/Tier I programs prepare candidates for P–12 leadership positions not limited to principalship (e.g., roles that include supervision and evaluation of personnel, coordination of instructional programs, management of school, district, or county fiscal services)	46 (M.A.) 37 (credential only)	65 (1 district-based cohort)	7 +2 adjuncts	10 credits

Table A.1—continued

University	Program Under Redesign	Degree/Endorsement for Certification	State Context	# of Program Credits	# of Students (Regional/District-Based Cohort)	# of Faculty	Clinical Experience Requirement
University of Connecticut	Administrator Preparation Program (all 3 tracks)	6th-year diploma/Connecticut Intermediate Administrator Certification	Intermediate certification allows holder to take on range of administrative positions, including department chair, assistant principal, principal, and assistant superintendent	35	90 (1 district-based cohort)	14	12 credits (structure varies among tracks)
Virginia State University	Educational Administration and Supervision	M.S., M.Ed., or doctoral degree/Level I Educational Administration and Supervision PreK–12 certification	Level I programs preparing candidates as school site administrator or central office supervisor	26	15 (0 district-based cohort)	3 + 2 adjuncts	90 days full-time
Western Kentucky University	Principal Preparation Program (P3; focus on Level I)	Ed.S./Kentucky provisional certification (Level I completion) or Professional certification (Level II completion)	Level I programs preparing candidates for positions as, assistant principals and principals	27 (Level 1) + 12 (Levels II)	75 (1 district-based cohort)	5 + 6 adjuncts	Course-embedded (Level I) + 6 credits (Level II)

SOURCES: Publicly available information—for example, program website and student handbooks, as well as interviews with the university's UL and/or program director.

NOTES: Ed.S. = education specialist; P–12 = preschool through 12th grade; M.A. = master of arts; M.S. = master of science; M.Ed. = master of education; MSA = master of school administration; NELA = Northeast Leadership Academy.

Table A.2
UPPI Sites

University	District/Consortium Partners	State Partner	Mentor Program(s)
Albany State University M2,[a] historically black public university in Albany, Georgia	**Calhoun County Schools** • 3 schools • 652 students • 98% minority • 95% FRPL • Rural	**Dougherty County School System** • 23 schools • 15,194 students • 92% minority • 100% FRPL • City	**Pelham City Schools** • 3 schools • 1,473 students • 63% minority[b] • 79% FRPL • Rural	Georgia Professional Standards Commission	Quality-Plus Leader Academy (QPLA) New York City Leadership Academy (NYCLA)
Florida Atlantic University R2, public university in Boca Raton, Florida	**Broward County Public Schools** • 353 schools • 269,098 students • 49% minority • 62% FRPL • Suburb: Large	**School District of Palm Beach County** • 277 schools • 189,322 students • 67% minority • 60% FRPL • Suburb: Large	**St. Lucie County Public Schools** • 51 schools • 40,045 students • 64% minority • 74% FRPL • City	Florida Department of Education	University of Denver
North Carolina State University R1, public, land-grant university in Raleigh, North Carolina	**Johnston County School District** • 46 schools • 34,857 students • 42% minority • 53% FRPL • Rural	**Northeast Leadership Academy (NELA) Consortium (13 districts)** • 140 schools • 60,119 students • 37%–95% minority • 80% FRPL • Rural	**Wake County Public School System** • 177 schools • 157,839 students • 53% minority • 34% FRPL • Suburb	North Carolina Department of Public Instruction	University of Denver
San Diego State University R2, public university in San Diego, California	**Chula Vista Elementary School District** • 47 schools • 30,230 students • 87% minority • 54% FRPL • Suburb	**San Diego City Unified School District** • 226 schools • 129,380 students • 77% minority • 59% FRPL • City	**Sweetwater Union High School District** • 31 schools • 41,050 students • 92% minority • 55% FRPL • Suburb	California Commission on Teacher Credentialing	University of Washington
University of Connecticut R1, public university in Storrs, Connecticut	**Hartford Public Schools** • 63 schools • 20,874 students • 94% minority • 78% FRPL • City	**Meriden Public Schools** • 17 schools • 7,927 students • 68% minority • 69% FRPL • Suburb	**New Haven Public Schools** • 44 schools • 21,631 students • 85% minority • 57% FRPL • City	Connecticut State Department of Education	University of Illinois at Chicago New York City Leadership Academy

Table A.2—continued

University	District/Consortium Partners			State Partner	Mentor Program(s)
Virginia State University M2, historically black, public, land-grant university in Petersburg, Virginia	Henrico County Public Schools • 81 schools • 51,534 students • 59% minority • 43% FRPL • Suburb	Hopewell City Public Schools • 7 schools • 4,376 students • 73% minority • 68% FRPL • Suburb	Sussex County Public Schools • 3 schools • 1,066 students • 80% minority • 72% FRPL • Rural	Virginia Department of Education	Quality-Plus Leader Academy
Western Kentucky University M1, public university in Bowling Green, Kentucky	Green River Regional Educational Cooperative (GRREC) The 43 member districts are spread across South Central Kentucky: • 349 schools • 149,836 students • Rural, town, suburb, and small city Initially, three of the member districts were involved in UPPI; two more districts joined in late 2017: Bowling Green Independent School District • 10 schools • 4,100 students • 41% minority • 53% FRPL • City Simpson County Schools • 6 schools • 3,037 students • 19% minority • 59% FRPL • Town	Daviess County Public Schools • 22 schools • 11,814 students • 16% minority • 52% FRPL • Suburb Warren County Public Schools • 35 schools • 15,066 students • 31% minority • 57% FRPL • Rural	Owensboro Public Schools • 13 schools • 5,150 students • 35% minority • 68% FRPL • City	Kentucky Education Professional Standards Board	University of Illinois at Chicago

SOURCES: The source for number of schools and students and urban/rural locale classification is the National Center for Education Statistics (U.S. Department of Education, 2017a). Data on student enrollment reflect the 2015–2016 school year. All other data reflect the 2016–2017 school years.

NOTE: FRPL = free or reduced-price lunch.

[a] According to the Carnegie Classification System (2017), colleges and universities are identified against specific criteria as *Research* (grant at least 20 doctoral degrees), *Master's* (grant at least 50 master's and fewer than 20 doctoral degrees), *Baccalaureate* (at least 50 percent baccalaureate or higher, fewer than 50 master's or 20 doctoral degrees), and *Baccalaureate/Associate's*. Research schools are further sorted into *R1* (highest research activity), *R2* (higher research activity), and *R3* (moderate research activity). Master's schools are further sorted into *M1* (larger), *M2* (medium), and *M3* (smaller).

[b] % minority = percentage of African-American, Hispanic, Asian, Native American/Hawaiian, and 2+ race students; % FRPL = percentage of students eligible for free- or reduced-price lunch. The source for percentage of minority students and students eligible for FPRL is the Office for Civil Rights' Civil Rights Data Collection survey conducted in 2013 (U.S. Department of Education, 2017b).

Albany State University

Program

Albany State University (ASU) was founded in 1903 and is one of three historically black colleges and universities in the University System of Georgia. It is located in Albany, a town of about 70,000 people; the region is otherwise rural and one of the most impoverished areas in the country. As of January 1, 2017, the university consolidated with Darton State College and saw unexpected, general declines in student enrollment.

ASU's Educational Leadership program is housed within the Department of Counseling and Educational Leadership in the College of Education. The program being redesigned under UPPI is the sixth-year Ed.S. program that confers the Ed.S. degree and certification to become a school principal or district administrator in Georgia. As of the 2015–2016 academic year, the Ed.S. program was aligned to the Georgia Education Leadership Standards. As of fall 2016, the Ed.S. program had 34 candidates and four full-time faculty members.

In accordance with state requirements, the Ed.S. program requires 30 to 36 graduate semester hours of course work in Educational Leadership and Supervision. Furthermore, students must complete 12 semester hours of graduate field experience and pass the Georgia Assessment for the Certification of Educators' Content Assessment in Educational Leadership.

Following state-determined criteria effective 2016, students entering ASU's Ed.S. program (see below), a Tier II program, must have at least a master's degree, be in a leadership role (assistant principal or higher), obtain recommendations that speak to the applicant's leadership potential from a direct supervisor and the superintendent, and provide evidence of successful performance in a leadership position. ASU specifically requires a minimum 3.0 grade point average (GPA) in the master's program and three years of leadership experience. There is strong desire from university and district leadership to recruit applicants that have served in southwest Georgia.

The Ed.S. program is primarily an in-person, performance-based program with a requirement of ten courses and 750 clinical hours. Students can choose to concentrate on building-level or system-level leadership. In the building-level leadership specialization, students are not only prepared for the basic managerial aspects of leading a school but also take courses specifically aimed at instructional management. In the system-level leadership specialization, students take courses that prepare them for administrative positions in the central office.

Students in both specializations complete clinical experiences, in a school or central office, respectively. Prior to July 2017, students could complete their clinical experiences solely at their current school. During the clinical assignment, students complete and document 15 performance-based tasks from a list of options. Four faculty members at ASU serve as clinical supervisors and observe students at their clinical experience sites. In addition, building principals or district administrative leaders serve as on-site mentors for the candidates.

District Partners

ASU trains leaders for 26 school systems in southwest Georgia. Among its three district partners for UPPI, two—Calhoun County School System (CCSS) and Pelham City Schools (PCS)—are rural school districts with which ASU has had no prior partnership. CCSS consists of three schools and 652 students, with 98 percent minority (i.e., nonwhite) and 95 percent of students eligible for the free and reduced-price lunch (FRPL) program. PCS has three schools and 1,473 students, with 63 percent minority and 78 percent of students eligible for FRPL. The other district—Dougherty County School System (DCSS)—operates 23 schools and learning centers and is one of the larger school districts in Georgia, with 15,194 students. About 92 percent of DCSS students are minority and eligible for FRPL. About 70 percent of DCSS school- or system-level leaders are ASU graduates.

State Landscape and Partner

The Georgia Professional Standards Commission (GaPSC) is Georgia's educator certification and educational program accrediting organization. Beginning in 2008, GaPSC required that educational leadership programs lead to an Ed.S. degree (rather than a master's degree) and that programs require a significant number of hours of clinical experience. In June 2015, the GaPSC adopted the Georgia Educational Leadership Standards, which are based on the PSEL and focus on instructional leadership.

Concurrent with but not influenced by UPPI, in October 2016, the GaPSC instituted a two-tier leader preparation system in the state. Tier 1 programs certify individuals entering a preschool through 12th grade (P–12) school-level position below the principal or a district-level position that does not involve supervision of principals. Tier II programs certify educators already in leadership positions (e.g., teacher leaders, coaches, assistant principals) advancing to principal, superintendent, or similar supervisory positions at the district level. For Tier 1 certification, candidates must complete the Georgia Assessments for the Certification of Educators (GACE) Ethics Exam and the GACE Leadership Assessment to receive their certification. Tier II certification does not require any assessments, but a program must address the Georgia Educational Leadership Standards through the clinical component, with supporting coursework. GaPSC's tiered system also emphasizes the role of school districts as partners in supporting program development and candidates.

Mentor Programs

Gwinnett County Public Schools district-developed principal development pipeline program, the Quality-Plus Leader Academy (QPLA), and the New York City Leadership Academy (NYCLA) are mentor programs for ASU. QPLA aims to improve student achievement by identifying and preparing highly effective leaders through their two programs, the Aspiring Leader Program and the Aspiring Principal Program. The other mentor program, NYCLA, is a nationally recognized nonprofit organization that supports and prepares school leaders. NYCLA's approach to leadership development includes hands-on and on-the-job learning, skill development, and continual self-reflection for educators to hone their leadership skills.

Florida Atlantic University

Program
Florida Atlantic University (FAU) opened in 1964 as the first public university in southeast Florida. FAU is a Research 2 institution on a suburban campus in Boca Raton. The Department of Educational Leadership and Research Methodology in the College of Education offers an M.Ed. degree in K–12 Educational Leadership with a Level 1 leadership certification, an Ed.S. degree in K–12 Educational Leadership with a leadership certification, a Florida Level 1 Certificate for those already holding a master's degree, and a doctoral degree (Ph.D.) in K–12 Educational Leadership. In 2015, there were 341 students in all of the principal preparation programs offered at FAU. Total enrollment across Level 1 leadership programs is about 150 students, with a faculty of some 20 full-time members, ten of whom are also school leaders. The FAU educational leadership program is the largest UPPI program in enrollment and faculty size.

Under UPPI, FAU is redesigning the M.Ed. program, an entry-level (Level 1) program that prepares individuals to be assistant or interim principals. This redesign is based on an existing program model, the Principal Rapid Orientation and Preparation in Educational Leadership (PROPEL) Program. The PROPEL program specifically prepares M.Ed. candidates for leadership positions in Broward County Public Schools (BCPS). PROPEL students form their own closed cohort, complete their clinical requirements exclusively at Broward County schools, and their curriculum is modified from the traditional curriculum with learning objectives that match the needs of BCPS. The traditional M.Ed. program, however, follows a curriculum that is not district-specific, and students may complete their clinical requirements at any district. FAU aims to expand PROPEL to additional district partners as well as its traditional M.Ed. program. But, program objectives, sequencing, and requirements are similar for FAU's traditional and PROPEL partnership programs.

The nonpartnership, traditional M.Ed. program with Level 1 certification is three semesters long and requires candidates to complete 33 credits of coursework in leadership foundations, research foundations, and professional knowledge as well as three semesters of an experiential learning/clinical experience. The clinical experience is a sustained experience in one school. As part of the application package to the program, students must secure the support of a building administrator willing to sponsor/ mentor the student for the entire three semesters of the clinical component. Students can complete many of these credits (excepting clinical experience credits) via multiple delivery modes, including "fast-track" courses offered on five to eight consecutive Saturdays in a given semester, online semester-long courses, and traditional, in-person semester-long courses.

With the partnership programs, both in the PROPEL program before UPPI and in the redesigned programs with all three districts under UPPI, the partner districts play a role in nominating candidates for the program. Like the traditional M.Ed. program, candidates must identify and secure sponsorship from their current school principal with whom they will complete the clinical experience component of the program. Students in the partnership programs complete the program in closed cohorts with other students from the same district. All M.Ed. candidates in both traditional and partnership programs must also pass the Florida Educational Leader Exam (FELE) to receive their degree. FELE is designed to measure prospective school administrators' achievement of the benchmarks established by the Florida State Board of Education: Leadership for Student Learning, Organizational Development, and Systems Leadership.

District Partners

FAU's three UPPI district partners are Broward County Public Schools (BCPS), the School District of Palm Beach County (SDPBC), and St. Lucie County School District (SLCSD). In 2011, FAU launched the PROPEL program in partnership with BCPS and with support from a U.S. Department of Education "Race to the Top" grant. So FAU and BCPS have a longstanding relationship. FAU launched a similar program to PROPEL in 2017 in partnership with SLCSD called Educational Leadership: Internship to Excellence (ELITE). SLCSD had, in the past, a strong partnership with FAU focused on teacher preparation. Under UPPI, FAU will launch a third partnership program with PBCS called Leadership for Excellence and Equity (EXEQ). SDPBC has had no prior partnership with FAU.

All three district partners in FAU's UPPI initiative are predominantly urban and suburban, but there are some relatively rural areas of the districts in the western parts of the counties. The three districts also serve a large proportion of minority (i.e., nonwhite) students; 60–74 percent of each district's students are eligible for FRPL. Whereas one of the district partners (SLCSD) serves a smaller student body (40,045 students), the other two district partners serve large student bodies of over 180,000 students. With UPPI, BCPS and FAU aim to improve the PROPEL program further and use PROPEL as a template and guide post for the ELITE and EXEQ programs.

State Landscape and Partner

Principal preparation programs and principal licensure in Florida are both required to meet state regulations and standards. The Division of Educator Quality in the Florida Department of Education is responsible for approving principal preparation programs in universities and principal licensure requirements in districts. Approved principal preparation programs require alignment with Florida's Principal Leadership Standards, Florida Professional Development Protocol Standards, and standards determined by the National Staff Development Council.

Florida has two types of principal licenses: Level 1, which prepares candidates to be assistant or interim principals, and Level 2, which prepares candidates to be school-building principals. Universities are primarily responsible for preparing candidates for Level 1 licenses. The districts, with some assistance from universities if requested, lead candidate preparation for Level 2. A law enacted in 2017 requires that candidates demonstrate instructional expertise and leadership potential to be admitted to Level 1 principal preparation programs. Individual universities have autonomy to determine how they will measure those requirements, however.

Mentor Program

The University of Denver's Educational Leadership and Policy Studies (ELPS) department in the Morgridge College of Education is the mentor program for both FAU and North Carolina State University). The department chair serves as the primary liaison to the two UPPI teams. The ELPS department offers several programs that integrate leadership with systems thinking, policy, and research, with particular focus on transformative/turnaround leadership. The department chair for ELPS brings expertise in redesigning principal preparation programs with district partners, having co-created and launched the Ritchie Program for School Leaders in conjunction with Denver Public Schools in 2002. The Ritchie Program for School Leaders is widely touted as a model principal preparation program and has similar elements to UPPI's redesign requirements, such as a rigorous selection process, curriculum grounded in the real-world experiences of principals, and a strong university-district partnership.

North Carolina State University

Program

Founded in 1887 as a land-grant college, North Carolina State University's (NC State's) main campus is located in Raleigh, North Carolina. NC State's Educational Leadership program is housed within the Department of Educational Leadership, Policy, and Human Development in the College of Education. The program under UPPI redesign is the Master of School Administration program that confers the MSA degree and certification to become an assistant principal, principal, or district administrator in North Carolina. NC State's MSA program has two separate tracks at the beginning of the initiative: the traditional, on-campus MSA program consisting of students who pay their own tuition and serve in nearby districts, and the Northeast Leadership Academy (NELA), which is an alternative licensure program focused specifically on serving rural, high-need districts in northeast North Carolina using grant, district, and state scholarship funds to fully fund the students. NELA works in tandem with district leaders to rigorously select principal candidates and requires candidates to complete performance assessments to demonstrate their leadership skills.

While both models are subject to UPPI redesign, more emphasis is placed on revitalizing the on-campus MSA program to reflect best practices from NELA. Both the traditional MSA program and NELA require students to complete 42 semester credit hours, 18 of which are dedicated to building-level clinical experiences. Prior to redesign, the programs aligned to North Carolina state standards, the North Carolina Standards for School Executives, the Standards for Advanced Programs in Educational Leadership adopted by the Educational Leadership Constituent Council, the Council for the Accreditation of Educator Preparation, the North Carolina 21st Century Standards, and the North Carolina Department of Public Instruction's leadership competencies. Both models are two-year programs.

The on-campus MSA program has traditionally served local districts where candidates self-select into the program. The traditional MSA program is two years, with an embedded clinical component that takes place throughout the program and an optional, full-time, state funded principal residency. Included in the on-campus program are students from a separate statewide Principal Fellows Program who complete their NC State coursework in one year, followed by a full-time, yearlong clinical experience. MSA candidates who do not participate in a full-time, state-funded residency complete their clinical experience requirements in the schools in which they are currently employed, while Principal Fellows are placed in a separate school in their district as determined by their district-level leaders. Most classes take place in-person on weeknights at NC State's main campus. The focus of the course content is balanced between managerial and operational (e.g., School Law and Organizational Management) and instructional leadership (e.g., Teacher Empowerment and Leadership). The program is organized around an outcome-based portfolio system where candidates must upload performance evidences (artifacts) aligned to each course. The field activities are directly integrated with the curriculum content (i.e., the performance evidence required to complete each course is tied to the overall internship experience threaded throughout the program). A separate university supervisor (typically not a course instructor) monitors the clinical experience experiences, which takes place concurrently with coursework.

The NELA program, which serves 13 districts, was founded in 2010 and runs closed cohorts of students through its two-year program. NELA requires candidates to participate in coursework focused on school turnaround for historically low-performing schools and offers additional activities, including retreats and specialized trainings. NELA also emphasizes project-based learning. For NELA candidates, the clinical experience is a full-time principal residency for those who hold a provisional administrator license in the second academic year of the program, during which candidates serve as assistant administrators in a school in their sending district. Placement is determined jointly by NELA directors and district leadership.

District and Consortium Partners

NC State's district partners for UPPI include Wake County Public School System (WCPSS), Johnston County Public Schools (JCPS), and the NELA consortium of 13 rural districts, with Edgecombe County Public Schools (ECPS) playing a lead role in the consortium. Wake County, where NC State is located, has one of the largest school districts in the country, serving more than 150,000 students across 177 schools. Across this urban/suburban district, 53 percent are nonwhite, and 34 percent of students are eligible for FRPL. WCPSS, located approximately 32 miles southeast of Wake County, is a midsize rural district serving 46 schools with about 34,857 students. Overall, 42 percent of JCPS students are nonwhite, and 53 percent are eligible for FRPL. ECPS, located approximately 67 miles northeast of Wake County, has 14 schools serving nearly 6,000 students. About 69 percent of students are nonwhite, and 83 percent of students are eligible for FRPL.

NC State has worked with each of the district partners in some capacity prior to UPPI, albeit to varying degrees. NC State has run closed cohorts of its principal preparation program for candidates from WCPSS and JCPS in the past, although no formal partnership existed with either district prior to UPPI. There is a strong network of professional relationships between NC State and JCPS, due to the presence of several NC State graduates in district leadership roles in Johnston County. NC State has worked formally in partnership with some districts in the NELA consortium since the program's founding in 2010. Specifically, ECPS has worked with NC State through a formal partnership for five years. About 60 to 70 percent of ECPS's administrative team are NELA graduates.

State Landscape and Partner

North Carolina's Department of Public Instruction (NCDPI) oversees approval of licensure-granting programs and, to a lesser extent, educator and administrator licensure in the state. It does so together with the NC State Board of Education (NCSBE), which is the policymaking body charged with setting policies and procedures for public schools administered through NCDPI. NCDPI comprehensively redesigned licensing standards in 2008, requiring all programs in the state to reapply for approval. Currently, approved traditional principal preparation programs must meet NCDPI's North Carolina Standards for School Executives. NCSBE and NCDPI are minimally involved in principal licensure, since candidates need only graduate from an approved program and be recommended for licensure by that program. Administrative candidates in the state are not required to pass an exam.

Mentor Program

As discussed above, the University of Denver supports both Florida Atlantic University and NC State.

San Diego State University

Program

Founded in 1897, San Diego State University (SDSU) is a public research university in San Diego, California. SDSU's principal preparation program is housed within the Department of Educational Leadership in the College of Education. The program under UPPI redesign is the Preliminary Administrative Services Credential/Master of Arts in PK–12 Educational Leadership program. This program offers two options leading to the California Preliminary Administrative Services Credential—credentialing-only (37 credits) or master's-plus-credential (46 credits). The credential-only program takes place over three semesters, or about 18 months; the master's-plus-credential takes place over five semesters or about two years. Both programs are aligned to the state standards, the California Administrator Performance Expectations. The credential-only option is available to individuals who hold an education-related master's degree from an accredited university with a GPA of 3.0 or above. The master's-plus-credential option requires an additional nine units of coursework beyond that required in the credential-only option and completion of an action research project. In 2015–2016, SDSU credentialed 65 principal candidates. Seven full-time faculty members served the program.

The program admits two cohorts each fall: a San Diego Unified School District (SDUSD) cohort of applicants nominated and co-selected by SDUSD, and a regional cohort of candidates employed in other public, charter, or private schools in the area. Candidates for the SDUSD cohort are nominated by their principal in an admissions process jointly facilitated by the university and the district. Candidates for both cohorts must hold a California clear credential,[1] have at least three years of certified teaching experience, and have earned at least a 3.0 GPA in undergraduate studies. Candidates are assessed by a review committee along the following dimensions: evidence of demonstrated leadership, quality of recommendations, GPA and Graduate Record Examination (GRE) scores (the latter is required for master's-plus candidates only), and successful teaching experiences. Each cohort has 20 to 30 admitted students. Within each

---

[1] *Clear* means that all education and program requirements for the credential have been met.

cohort, candidates pursuing credential-only or master's-plus-credential options move through the program together.

SDSU's program is primarily delivered in-person through evening classes and seminars. The coursework includes content on both managerial and operational leadership and instructional leadership. The clinical component of the program is part-time and is aligned with the course scope and sequence, taking place concurrently through activities that candidates are required to engage in at their school sites. This fieldwork is structured around the identification of a problem of practice related to increasing student achievement for a target group and leading a site-based advisory committee through the development and implementation of a school improvement plan. Candidates are supervised by both a site-based administrator and a university-based clinical advisor (a doctoral candidate in SDSU's educational leadership program). Candidates must pass a comprehensive oral exam upon completion of core coursework to be recommended for the credential.

District Partners

SDSU trains aspiring school leaders for a range of school settings across the 42 districts within San Diego County and beyond. It is partnering with three districts for UPPI: SDUSD, Sweetwater Union High School District (SUHSD), and Chula Vista Elementary School District (CVESD). Among the three district partners for UPPI, SDUSD is the largest, serving more than 129,000 students across 226 schools in the 2016–2017 school year. SDUSD, located within a large city, is one of the largest school districts in the country and is the second largest in California. SDUSD serves a large Hispanic/Latino community (47 percent of its students). Fifty-nine percent of its students are eligible for FRPL. The other two district partners, SUHSD and CVESD, are smaller districts located about 10 miles south of the city of San Diego. SUHSD has 41,050 students across 31 schools, and CFESD serves 30,230 students across 47 schools. Both are large suburban districts. SUHSD students are 65 percent Hispanic/Latino, and 55 percent are eligible for FRPL. CVESD is 68 percent Hispanic/Latino, and 54 percent of students are eligible for FRPL. CVESD is one of four elementary school districts that feed into SUHSD. As such, district leaders in both districts regularly partner together on initiatives.

SDSU's principal preparation program has had a defined partnership with SDUSD since 2010, while the partnership to train aspiring leaders in the other two districts is new with UPPI. Moreover, the UPPI leadership team includes individuals with long-standing professional relationships with SDUSD. Several of the district leaders involved in UPPI are graduates of the Educational Leadership doctoral program at SDSU. SDUSD leaders have also taught as clinical faculty in SDSU's principal preparation program. Faculty members at SDSU have been formally involved in supporting the professional development for sitting principals in at least one district.

State Landscape and Partner

The California Commission on Teacher Credentialing (CTC) plays a role in both the approval and accreditation of Administrative Services programs and the credentialing of school administrators. After initial program approval, the Committee on Accreditation within the CTC reviews approved programs on a seven-year accreditation cycle. Programs are assessed against CTC's Preliminary Administrative Services Credential Program Standards, which are aligned to the California Administrator Performance Expectations (CAPEs). The CAPEs outline performance expectations for novice administrators in the state and are further aligned to the California Professional Standards for Education Leaders (CPSELs). CPSELs outlines expectations for administrators in the state more broadly. SDSU's accreditation review is scheduled for 2017–2018 under all these standards.

California has a two-tier credentialing system for school administrators. First, candidates must have a minimum of five years of teaching experience and must earn a preliminary credential by completing a commission-approved program (or clinical experience) or achieving a passing score on the California Preliminary Administrative Credential Examination. CTC is currently rolling out a performance assessment that will be required for candidates going through an approved program. Once individuals with a preliminary credential are hired into an administrative role, they have five years to clear their credential. This requires serving in a full-time administrative role for at least two years and completing a commission-approved administrative services induction program.

Mentor Program

The University of Washington (UW) supports SDSU through its Danforth Educational Leadership Program, a leader preparation program for principals and program administrators. The Danforth Educational Leadership Program prepares educators for leadership roles in P–12 school systems using an innovative competency-based program. The program offers principal certification, program administrator certification, or both, and a master's degree in education. UW has two dedicated staff that support SDSU, the Director of the Danforth Educational Leadership Program (and the Associate Dean of Professional Studies) and a consultant (or subcontractor). The consultant previously worked with SDSU on their performance assessments. UW primarily serves as a thought partner for SDSU and facilitates work on their key focus areas, such as "five kinds of thinking" for graduates, which pushes students beyond the typical standards and encourages innovation and creativity. UW also engages SDSU by encouraging and assisting them with exploring other possibilities for the program, such as having students conduct school site visits.

University of Connecticut

Program

The University of Connecticut (UCONN) is the state's flagship university and a Research 1 institution. The program under UPPI redesign, UCONN's Administrator Preparation Program (UCAPP), is housed within the Neag School of Education's Department of Educational Leadership. UCAPP is the largest academic program in the department, with about 90 students enrolled in 2016–2017, and the second-largest principal preparation program in the UPPI. Students are supported by approximately 14 full-time tenure-track or clinical faculty members, 12 adjunct faculty, four clinical supervisors, and more than 60 mentor principals. The 35-credit post-master program leads to a sixth-year diploma, and program graduates are eligible for the Connecticut Intermediate Administrator Certification, which is the license required of principals and other school administrators in the state.

The UCAPP program has two to three tracks or models of delivery: Traditional, Preparing Leaders of Urban Schools (PLUS; available in Hartford and New Haven), and Residency (when state funding is available)—all of which are subject to redesign under UPPI. All three tracks are cohort-based. The Traditional track is the university, course-based model typical of educator preparation programs across the country. Candidates apply as individuals to join one of three regional cohorts formed each year, for a maximum total of about 45 traditional-track students. A cohort progresses through the 35-credit, two-year program, following a prescribed sequence of standards-aligned courses and experiences. Key course concepts include school leadership and administration, supervision of educational organizations, program evaluation for school improvement, and (positive) school climate. All UCAPP students, including traditional-track students, must complete 540 hours of clinical training over the two-year program. The clinical experiences may take place at students' own school or their supervising principal's school. In addition to completing tasks and receiving mentoring, students must also schedule a minimum of five "Triad Meetings" with their site-based supervisor and university-based mentor principal over the course of their program of study.

The second track in the UCAPP program is PLUS. This track has been preparing cohorts of leaders specifically for Hartford Public Schools (HPS) for five years and a cohort of leaders for the New Haven Public Schools (NHPS) since fall 2016. Each PLUS program enrolls cohorts of a maximum 15 students. (Candidates from nonpartner school districts may receive special permission to join a cohort.) Coursework is delivered in a modular, spiraling curriculum structure. Key concepts include instructional leadership, talent management, organizational leadership, and community engagement. The clinical experiences for these candidates is similar to that of traditional-track students. The main difference is that PLUS students receive ten clinical experience release days annually and must also complete a portfolio documenting their progress and what they have learned in the program's key content areas.

The last track, the Residency, aims to prepare principals to lead school turnaround. Residency applicants must work in districts partnering with LEAD CT, a 2013 consortium of mostly Connecticut-based educational organizations to support principal preparation and development in low-performing districts and schools. This model is distinct in that students take up a yearlong residency: They serve as an assistant principal for four days a week in a district designated as high priority for improvement and attend class on the fifth day. During the program, they retain their full teacher salary. In addition, Residency students receive half-tuition reimbursement from LEAD CT to encourage them to pursue leadership roles in the lowest-performing schools. The Residency model is jointly funded by the state department of education and the school district. Unlike in the other tracks, Residency students serve their clinical experience typically at one school over one academic year. In lieu of reflection journals and portfolios, Residency students file summary reports after each site visit from a Residency program coordinator. (As of 2017–2018—after the start of UPPI—the Residency track has been discontinued in indefinitely due to budget restrictions from the state.)

Regardless of track, all students go through a selective admission process that includes performance-based tasks. While traditional track students may apply to the program on their own, PLUS and Residency track students must have a nomination from their current principal, supervisor, or superintendent. PLUS students must also have extensive experience in either HPS or NHPS (or other districts with special permission).

District Partners

UCONN's district partners include Hartford Public Schools (HPS), New Haven Public Schools (NHPS), and Meriden Public Schools (MPS). As of 2015, HPS employed about 45 principals and 40 assistant principals and enrolled approximately 21,000 students. About 50 and 30 percent of those students were Hispanic/Latino and black, respectively, and about 78 percent of students were eligible for FRPL. NHPS is comparable to HPS in most ways. It has about 50 principals and 60 assistant principals and serves just about 21,000 students. It is also racially and ethnically diverse, with about 40 percent each Hispanic/Latino and black students. Compared with HPS, only 57 percent of its student body is eligible for FRPL. Finally, MPS is a suburban district that employs about 12 principals and 16 assistant principals. It has the smallest student body of the three district partners, serving about 9,000 students. Despite its smaller size, the MPS student body is as diverse and economically disadvantaged as that of the other districts. About 49 and 14 percent of its students are Hispanic/Latino and black, respectively. About 70 percent of its students qualify for FRPL.

State Landscape and Partner

The Connecticut State Department of Education (CSDE) is responsible for establishing and enforcing policies and guidelines for the accreditation of principal preparation programs and principal licensing in the state. The department's Bureau of Educator Standards and Certification specifically oversees the accreditation and certification processes. While state guidelines only require 18 credits of coursework for a principal preparation program (clinical experience is not required), few programs in the state offer an endorsement with fewer than 30 credits. Improving principal preparation and the quality of school leaders are among the CSDE's recent priorities. For example, in 2012, the CSDE established the Connecticut School Leadership Standards, comprising six performance expectations for leaders' skills, knowledge, and dispositions. Launched in 2013, another recent major initiative for CSDE is LEAD CT, which led directly to the development of UCAPP's Residency track, among other programs. CSDE also is developing a data dashboard as part of an initiative to transform educator preparation in the state (Network for Transforming Educator Preparation). The public dashboard will allow state leaders and other stakeholders to examine the performance of programs within a university department, including principal preparation programs.

Mentor Programs

University of Illinois at Chicago (UIC) supports UCONN to prepare effective principals by advising or serving as a thought partner in the development of curriculum, cultivating university-district partnerships, and developing state policy and standards. UIC received the Exemplary Leadership Preparation Program Award in 2013 from the University Council for Educational Administration for being a model principal preparation program and the Urban Impact Award from the Council of Great City Schools in 2012. The Urban Impact Award honored UIC for their positive impact on student learning through their partnership with the school district. UIC has been focused on preparing transformation leaders since 2002 and worked with The Wallace Foundation prior to UPPI. UIC partnered with Chicago Public Schools (CPS) on a project in which The Wallace Foundation funded a principal development project for Illinois and CPS. In that capacity, UIC worked with CPS to ensure their principal preparation program addressed CPS schools' needs. In addition to this relationship, UIC joined a task force for the Illinois principal development project co-funded by The Wallace Foundation and sponsored by Illinois's Board of Higher Education to refigure Illinois principal preparation. UIC has experience as a research-intensive institution that has a rich history examining and implementing principal preparation programs. In addition to UIC, UCONN selected New York City Leadership Academy (NYCLA) as a mentor program to support their clinical experience redesign. NYCLA supports both ASU and UCONN. See NYCLA's profile included in ASU section above.

Virginia State University

Program

Virginia State University (VSU) is a historically black, public land-grant university founded in 1882. VSU was the United States' first fully state-supported four-year institution of higher learning for African Americans. The Department of Educational Leadership within VSU's College of Graduate Studies offers an M.S., an M.Ed., and a doctoral degree in Educational Administration and Supervision. The two master's programs have the same core course requirements, and both can lead to licensure as a school administrator in Virginia; the M.S. degree requires an additional thesis paper. Under UPPI, VSU is redesigning the two master's programs (referred to as M.S./M. Ed.). The M.S/M.Ed. programs require candidates to complete 36 semester hours of coursework (12 courses) and pass the statewide assessment, the School Leader Licensure Assessment. As of 2016–2017, 15 students were enrolled in the M.S./M.Ed. programs in Educational Administration and Supervision.

In terms of recruitment and selection, candidates seeking admissions must complete a graduate application, hold a professional five-year renewable teaching license for the state of Virginia, present a recent competitive GRE score, provide a reflective personal essay describing educational leadership aspirations, have an undergraduate GPA of at least 2.8, and have three letters of recommendation from individuals familiar with the candidate's experience as an educational leader. Candidates may be admitted provisionally for one semester or six hours of coursework prior to submission of GRE scores or for those who do not meet the minimum GPA requirement or may be granted provisional acceptance followed by a review after completion of one semester or six hours of coursework. The Program Areas Admissions Committee reviews each applicant for admissions and makes recommendations to the Graduate Admissions Committee. The program currently offers fall, spring, and summer admissions.

The Educational Administration and Supervision program consists of 12 courses. Three prerequisite courses focus on foundations of education, education research, and statistics in education. Nine core courses focus on school improvement and instruction, leader development, community involvement and engagement, and school law and ethics. The nine core courses are taken in a specific sequence and require in-course fieldwork experiences separate from the full-time internship experience. Candidates are required to acquire a minimum of 12 hours of in-course field experience during each of the nine core courses, for a minimum of 140 hours total. These in-course field experiences take place both at the school of the candidate's employment as well as other schools. In terms of assessments, there is a common course assessment for each course and a culminating program-level written and oral comprehensive exam taken during the final semester of enrollment.

Certification and licensure requires a full-time, 90-day administrative clinical experience where the candidate serves in a leadership capacity in a school setting over a summer. The candidate is exposed to day-to-day operations as a leader while experiencing direct field leadership responsibilities and duties. Candidates are placed into schools based on an interview process with neighboring school divisions. Candidates are required to obtain a minimum of 260 clinical experience hours. Throughout the clinical experience, candidates are required to engage in specific activities, including writing professional development plans, conducting school safety audits, analyzing school climate, analyzing school budget, and collaborating with families.

District Partners

A large proportion of school administrators in central Virginia are graduates of VSU's principal preparation program, including many at the UPPI partner districts: Henrico County Public Schools (Henrico PCS), Hopewell City Public Schools (Hopewell CPS), and Sussex County Public Schools (SCPS). Henrico CPS is the largest of the three partners, with 81 schools serving a total of 51,534 students, and is the least disadvantaged of the three divisions, with 59 percent minority (i.e., nonwhite) students and 43 percent of students receiving FRPL. Comparatively smaller, Hopewell CPS includes six schools serving 4,376 students. Hopewell CPS's student population consists of 73 percent minority students, and 68 percent of the students receive FRPL. SCPS has just three schools serving 1,066 students. SCPU serves the most disadvantaged students of the three districts, with 80 percent minority students and 72 percent of students receiving FRPL. Henrico CPS did not have a prior relationship with VSU, beyond hiring VSU graduates. Hopewell CPS has had a strong relationship with VSU due to its proximity to the university and personal connections—many members of the staff teach at VSU. SCPS has worked with VSU in the past, with VSU providing graduate courses to district staff.

State Landscape and Partner

The Virginia Department of Education's (VDOE's) Division of Teacher Education and Licensure is responsible for school personnel preparation programs and licensing. Approved principal preparation programs must align with the Educational Leadership Council Consortium standards. New regulations will soon require each institution and principal preparation program to be accredited through the Council for the Accreditation of Educator Preparation (CAEP) and to meet CAEP standards for principal preparation. VDOE is exploring opportunities to move toward competency-based programs that require students to pass standardized exams under the new standards.

VDOE has a two-tiered principal preparation licensing system. Level I is required to serve as a building-level administrator or central office supervisor; Level II is an optional endorsement for an experienced building-level administrator.

Mentor Program

Quality Plus Leadership Academy (QPLA) supports both ASU and VSU. See QPLA's profile included in ASU section above.

Western Kentucky University

Program

Western Kentucky University (WKU) is a large Master's 1, public university founded in 1906 in Bowling Green, Kentucky. WKU's flagship Principal Preparation Program (P3) is the subject of redesign under UPPI. This program is housed within the Department of Educational Administration, Leadership, and Research in the College of Education and Behavioral Sciences and leads to school principal certification. Since 2013, P3 has been cohort-based, with an average of 25 enrollees per cohort. These include students enrolled in one of three ways: through the main campus; through Leading to Learn, an i3 grant partnership with the Green River Regional Educational Cooperative; and through a cohort based at WKU's regional campus in Owensboro. The P3 is served by four full-time faculty members who all have held P–12 administrative positions previously, as well as adjunct faculty members drawn from practicing principals, superintendents, or state-level officials.

The certification program requires a total of 30 credit hours plus 9 hours of co-requisites. Students take 18 hours of initial core classes over three semesters plus 9 hours of co-requisites to earn a five-year, Level I Statement of Eligibility. This allows candidates to obtain employment as assistant principals or principals. Not included in the UPPI redesign, Level II certification must be completed within five years of Level I completion and can be pursued regardless of whether a candidate is employed in a school leadership position. Level II certification requires 12 additional credit hours, half of which must take place in a site-based clinical experience. Candidates must also pass the Kentucky Principal Specialty Test and the School Leaders Licensure Assessment test.

Following mandates established by the Education Professional Standards Board for all principal preparation programs in Kentucky, P3's minimum admission requirements include a master's degree prior to matriculation with 3.0 coursework GPA, three years of teaching experience, and a current teaching certificate. Interested candidates apply for admissions based on a standard program application and are selected by the Principal Preparation Admissions Committee. The program admits both Fall and Spring cohorts. For Level I candidates, WKU currently runs both open and closed cohorts. Any individual can self-select into open cohorts, whereas only candidates from specific districts gain admittance to closed cohorts.

P3 requires admitted students to complete required content areas in coursework and administers mandatory assessments that align with state standards for principal preparation. The P3 Level I certification program is characterized by in-person and online components. Level I certification requires six core courses structured with two courses per term over the course of three semesters. Fieldwork is embedded in all six courses. These courses must be taken sequentially and cover topics including building school culture, staff development, organizational structures, and more. Courses have performance-based assessments. Currently, Level I certification does not require an official internship. Relevant principal experiences are obtained through fieldwork embedded within the core courses.

District and Consortium Partners

At the start of UPPI, The Green River Regional Educational Cooperative (GRREC) provided resources, training, and professional development to 43 school districts in south central and western Kentucky. (By fall 2018, it has grown to support 45 school districts.) WKU's Department of Educational Administration, Leadership, and Research has a long-standing relationship with GRREC. The dean of the college is on GRREC's board of directors, and the two organizations have partnered on multiple grants, including the Leading to Learn initiative designed to provide quality professional learning opportunities to aspiring and practicing principals. In addition to grant funding, GRREC is funded primarily by membership fees from districts.

Altogether, at the start of UPPI, GRREC's 43 member districts employ about 295 principals and 233 assistant principals. WKU estimates that about two-thirds to three-quarters of practicing school administrators in the GRREC region are program alumni. The large majority of GRREC member districts serve rural communities, and at least 50 percent of students qualify for FRPL in all GRREC districts.

The UPPI initiative engaged three districts at the outset: Bowling Green Independent School District (BGISD), Owensboro Public Schools (OPS), and Simpson County Schools (SCS). The three districts vary in the percentage of minority (i.e., nonwhite) students they serve; BGISD serves 41 percent, OPS serves 35 percent, and SCS serves 19 percent. The percentage of students who qualify for FRPL varies less; BGISD has 53 percent, OPS has 68 percent, and SCS has 59 percent. Unlike most of GRREC districts, these three are not rural. BGISD and OPS are located in small cities, and SCS is in a designated "town." As of July 2017, Warren County Public Schools, one of the largest county school districts in GRREC, with 35 schools serving more than 15,000 students, joined the initiative. And in fall 2017, another large district, Daviess County Public Schools, with 22 schools and almost 12,000 students, was preparing to join. WKU intends to engage additional district partners over the life of the UPPI.

State Landscape and Partner

The Kentucky Education Professional Standards Board (EPSB) is an independent agency that, among other responsibilities, oversees accreditation of educator and administrator preparation programs as well as the certification of teachers and administrators. In August 2018, EPSB became an agency housed in the Kentucky Department of Education. In addition to receiving national accreditation through the National Council for Accreditation in Teacher Education, WKU's P3 must receive renewed approval from EPSB every seven years. The EPSB has the authority to approve curriculum materials (including admissions criteria, required coursework, and target outcomes) as well as to establish policies that affect program design (including minimum contact hours, supervisor credentials, and reporting processes related to field experiences).

As mentioned above, Kentucky has a two-tiered leader preparation system. Level I certification enables students to obtain a provisional certificate to become a school leader, whereas Level II certification serves as a certification renewal. Level II certification also enables students to satisfy Rank I requirements and obtain a professional certificate. Satisfying Rank I allows school leaders to receive a pay increase.

Mentor Program

The University of Illinois at Chicago supports both UCONN and WKU. See UIC's profile included in UCONN section above.

Policy Context

Professional Standards for Educational Leaders and National Educational Leadership Preparation Standards

In 2015, the National Policy Board for Educational Administration (NPBEA) approved the 2015 Professional Standards for Educational Leaders (PSEL). PSEL are research-based and also based on real experiences of school leaders. They are designed to set high expectations for preparing and evaluating school leaders of all levels, including principals and assistant principals. Their goal is to ensure that district and school leaders improve student achievement (NPBEA, 2015). PSEL are intended for use by state boards of education to inform their policy and practices around school leader licensure and professional development (NPBEA, 2015).

PSEL centers on "ten interdependent domains, qualities, and values of leadership work that research and practice suggest are integral to student success" (NPBEA, 2015, p. 3):

- mission, vision, and core values
- ethics and professional norms
- equity and cultural responsiveness
- curriculum, instruction, and assessment
- community of care and support for students
- professional capacity of school personnel
- professional community for teachers and staff
- meaningful engagement of families and community
- operations and management
- school improvement.

Ultimately, school leaders should strive to ensure that every student's academic success and well-being are being addressed by way of fulfilling these standards (NPBEA, 2015).

To complement PSEL, new standards for school leader preparation programs to replace the Educational Leadership Constituencies Council standards of 2011 have also been developed. The National Educational Leadership Preparation (NELP) standards (University Council for Educational Administration, 2018), available for use beginning January 2018, align with PSEL, but offer greater specificity around what is expected of preparation program graduates and new educational leaders at the building and district levels. For example, NELP for building-level leaders is framed around seven standards that encapsulate the PSEL standards; in addition, an eighth standard addresses the requirements related to clinical practice. In sum, NELP speaks to the quality of educational leader preparation programs and will be used by the Council for the Accreditation of Educator Preparation to review and approve such preparation programs.

Every Student Succeeds Act

In late 2015, Congress passed the Every Student Succeeds Act (ESSA; Pub. L. 114-95, 2015). ESSA provides states with substantially greater autonomy in their use of federal resources for education, as well as greater opportunities to support school leadership improvement. States developed consolidated state ESSA plans, with the input of their stakeholders as required by the law, and submitted the plans to the U.S. Department of Education in either April or November 2017. ESSA planning was concurrent with the first year of UPPI, providing an unusual opportunity for preparation programs and their districts to engage with state partners about the direction of principal preparation in the state. The confluence of events also provided state policymakers with ready access to educators who had been thinking deeply about how to improve school leadership. The relationship between ESSA and UPPI will be explored more fully in the special topic report for this evaluation.

Data Collection

This appendix provides details on data collection and analysis. It details the site visits conducted in spring 2017 and fall 2017, providing details about the number of data collection activities and participants by role. We also provide a snapshot of our data collection protocols.

Site Visit Planning

Planning for the first site visit began in late 2016 to early 2017, when we conducted introductory phone calls with the UL and other key members of the UPPI team for each site. Next, we provided the UL materials to plan the visit: categories of respondents to include in data collection, scheduling guidance, a sample site visit schedule, and recruitment materials (i.e., project abstract, recruitment email, consent handout) to forward to potential respondents. The UL and project manager/administrative assistant, if available, helped schedule the data collection activities (i.e., interviews and focus groups) and recruit and confirm participants. We communicated regularly with the UL (or project manager/administrative assistant) to respond to questions and concerns.

Spring 2017 Site Visit

Between March and May 2017, a two-person team visited each of the sites for three to four days to conduct interviews (target length of 60–75 minutes) and focus groups (target length of 75–90 minutes) with participants representing the university, the district partners/consortium, the state partner organization, and the mentor programs. As needed, we conducted phone or video conferences to complete the planned data collection.

Table C.1 presents a snapshot of our spring 2017 data collection. In total, across the seven sites, we completed 103 data collection activities (with an average of 15 inter-

Table C.1
Summary of Spring 2017 Site Visit Data Collection

Site	# of Interviews (60–75 minutes each) Involving Individuals in Each Role (# of Participants)					# of Focus Groups (75–90 minutes each) Involving Persons in Each Role (# of Participants)[a]					# of Data Collection Activities Completed (# of Participants)
	ULs and Program Leads UL, Key Faculty	University Administrator Provost, Dean	District Partner Leads (Associate) Superintendent, Chief Academic Officer	State Partner Leads Division Director, Chief Talent Officer	Mentor Program Leads Director, Coordinator, Vice-President	UPPI Leadership Team Typically persons participating in individual interviews	Research Faculty Tenure-track faculty teaching in program	Adjunct/ Clinical Faculty Often practitioners from districts, teaching in program	Mentor Principals Site-based principals in partner districts supervising candidates in program	Principal Candidates 2016 program enrollees, not necessarily from partner districts	
ASU	2 (2)	1 (1)	3 (4)	1 (1)	2 (4)	1 (12)	1 (3)	0	0	1 (6)	12 (33)
FAU	2 (2)	1 (4)	3 (11)	1 (6)	1 (1)	1 (10)	1 (6)	1 (5)	3 (26)	2 (20)	16 (91)
NC State	2 (2)	1 (1)	3 (5)	1 (2)	1 (1)	1 (9)	1 (2)	2 (8)	3 (15)	1 (5)	16 (50)
SDSU	1 (1)	1 (1)	4 (4)	1 (1)	1 (1)	1 (5)	1 (8)	1 (4)	2 (4)	1 (8)	14 (37)
UCONN	3 (3)	1 (1)	3 (6)	1 (2)	1 (3)	1 (9)	1 (2)	1 (7)	3 (4)	1 (8)	16 (45)
VSU	1 (2)	1 (2)	3 (6)	1 (3)	1 (4)	1 (9)	1 (2)	1 (1)	0	1 (4)	11 (33)
WKU	2 (2)	2 (2)	4 (4)	1 (1)	1 (1)	1 (6)	2 (4)	0	4 (15)	1 (7)	18 (42)
Total	13 (14)	8 (12)	23 (40)	7 (16)	8 (15)	7 (60)	8 (27)	6 (25)	15 (64)	8 (58)	103 (331)

[a] In some cases, participants were part of multiple data collection activities and are double-counted in the table. For example, the UL is counted for both the individual interview and also the UPPI leadership team focus group, and a research faculty member may have been part of both the UPPI leadership team and the research faculty focus group. Note also that, in some cases, because of scheduling difficulty, faculty, mentor principals, or candidates were interviewed individually. Nevertheless, for the purpose of the tally, such individuals are considered participants in a (intended) focus group.

views and focus groups combined per site). Across the seven sites, we spoke with 331 individuals[1] (average 47 per site).

By role, we spoke with

- 7 ULs
- 6 program leads (e.g., key program faculty who are not ULs)
- 8 university administrators (e.g., dean or provost)
- 23 district partner leads (e.g., superintendent or designate)
- 7 state partner leads
- 8 mentor program leads.

We also conducted various types of focus groups. We aimed to conduct at least one focus group with each type of participant. In some cases, we held additional focus groups to capture unique perspectives. For example, at Florida Atlantic University, North Carolina State University, San Diego State University, and the University of Connecticut, we held separate mentor principal focus groups for each partner district or program track, to better understand the mentoring arrangements:

- 7 with UPPI leadership teams
- 8 with research faculty
- 6 with adjunct faculty
- 15 focus groups with site-based mentor/supervising principals
- 8 focus groups with candidates who enrolled in the principal preparation program under redesign in the 2016–2017 academic year. The candidates did not have to be associated with one of the partner districts, so all districts were not necessarily represented. Moreover, at this stage of UPPI, not all partner districts had principal candidates enrolled in the program.

Fall 2017 Site Visit

Table C.2 presents a snapshot of our fall 2017 data collection. In total, across the seven sites, we completed 73 data collection activities (with an average of 10 interviews and focus groups combined per site). Across the seven sites, we spoke with 180 individuals[2] (average 26 per site).

---

[1]   In some cases, participants were part of multiple data collection activities and are double-counted. See detailed note for Table A.1.

[2]   In some cases, participants were part of multiple data collection activities and are double-counted. See detailed note for Table B.1.

Table C.2
Summary of Fall 2017 Site Visit Data Collection

Site	# of Interviews (60–75 min each) Involving Individuals in Each Role (# of Participants)				UPPI Leadership Team Meeting Observation (# of Participants[a])	# of Data Collection Activities Completed (# of Participants[a])
	ULs and Program Leads *UL, Key Faculty*	**District Partner Leads and Subgroup Leads** *(Associate) Superintendent, Chief Academic Officer, Information Technology Specialist, etc.*	**State Partner Leads and Subgroup Leads** *Division Director, Chief Talent Officer*	**Mentor Program Leads** *Director, Coordinator, Vice-President*	**UPPI Leadership Team Members** *Typically persons participating in individual interviews*	
ASU	2 (2)	4 (5)	1 (1)	2 (3)	1 (21)	10 (32)
FAU	4 (6)	4 (6)	1 (5)	1 (1)	1 (13)	11 (31)
NC State	4 (5)	5 (8)	1 (3)	1 (1)	1 (12)	12 (29)
SDSU	4 (4)	4 (4)	1 (1)	1 (1)	1 (19)	11 (29)
UCONN	4 (5)	4 (5)	1 (1)	1 (2)	1 (7)	11 (20)
VSU	1 (1)	3 (3)	1 (2)	1 (1)	0 (0)	6 (7)
WKU	3 (3)	6 (8)	1 (2)	1 (2)	1 (17)	12 (32)
Total	22 (26)	30 (39)	7 (15)	8 (11)	7 (89)	73 (180)

[a] In some cases, participants were part of multiple data collection activities and are double-counted in the table. For example, the UL is counted for both the individual interview and also the UPPI Leadership Team Meeting Observation.

By role, we spoke with

- 7 ULs
- 19 program leads (e.g., key program faculty who are not ULs)
- 39 district partner leads or subgroup leads (e.g., Superintendent or designate)
- 15 state partner leads
- 11 mentor program leads.

We did not seek to speak with university administrators (e.g., dean or provost) in the fall, nor did we conduct focus groups. We did, however, conduct an observation of a UPPI leadership team meeting.

Regular Check-Ins

Table C.3 shows the data we collected as part of the regular (e.g., monthly) check-in phone calls we conducted with the UL at each site. On average, we spoke with the UL four times between site visits. We also attempted to check in regularly with district partner leads via phone, email, or online survey.

The check-in protocol consisted of seven questions. We sought updates about the key tasks the UPPI leadership team worked on in the past month, any new tools, processes, or strategies used to manage the change process, and extent of partner engage-

Table C.3
April–December 2017 Regular Check-In Data Collection

	# of Check-Ins Involving Individuals in Each Role		# of Data Collection Activities Completed
Site	UL	District Partner Leader (Associate) Superintendent, Chief Academic Officer	
ASU	5	6 (3/2/1 from each district)	11
FAU	4	6 (1/2/3 from each district)	10
NC State	3	3 (2/1/0 from each district)	6
SDSU	6	9(3/5/1 from each district)	15
UCONN	5	6 (3/2/1 from each district)	11
VSU	2	1 (1/0/0 from each district)	3
WKU	4	9 (6 from cooperative; 2/1/0 from each district)	13
Total	29	40	69

ment. We also elicited a challenge and a success the team encountered during the past month.

Data Collection Protocols

We developed interview, focus group, and team meeting observation protocols to guide thorough data collection.

Interview and Focus Group Protocol

The topics covered in the protocols for interviews and focus groups varied according to the target participant. In general, we sought information to understand the institutional context and to address the four research questions. For example, for program change, we asked about the program-specific UPPI theory of change; university principal preparation program features at baseline, prior to redesign; and planned changes to the program. For management of the redesign process, we elicited strategies, processes, and tools for managing the work, and partners' perceptions of the clarity of their roles. For partner engagement, we probed on the extent of each partner's engagement in the UPPI. Finally, for challenges and solutions, we sought to document organizational factors at all levels that might pose as barriers to the improvement effort. Table C.4 presents a sample of questions included in our protocols for the spring and fall 2017 site visits.

Table C.4
Sample Questions from Spring and Fall 2017 Site Visit Protocols

Research Question	Sample Questions	Respondent/Protocols
Background/ context	• What is your role in the UPPI? • What motivated you/your organization to think about redesigning the principal preparation program?	• ULs • University administrators • State partner leads
	• Please describe the hiring environment for principals/assistant principals in your district. • What current district policies or standards do you believe support the UPPI work? How?	• District partner leads
	• Historically what has been the [state organization's] role with respect to influencing/shaping principal preparation and development?	• State partner leads
	• What is your organization's prior experience with principal preparation program redesigns?	• Mentor program leads
	• What are the work conditions like as a principal in your district?	• Mentor principals
Program change	• Can you tell us about the curriculum for the principal preparation/education leadership program prior to any program redesign? • What curriculum changes have been planned so far as a result of the UPPI? • Can you describe the application, recruitment, and selection strategies prior to any program redesign?	• ULs • Research faculty • Adjunct faculty
	• Describe the typical clinical learning experience or internship with [program].	• ULs • Faculty • Mentor principals
	• What do you regard as the priorities for the UPPI team this year?	• UPPI leadership team
	• To what extent do you think the content covered by the course prepares candidates to take on an internship and eventually a principalship?	• Research faculty • Adjunct faculty • Mentor principals • Principal candidates
Management of the redesign process	• To what extent do you believe the partners have common/shared goals for the UPPI project? • To what extent do you believe the various partners are clear about their roles and responsibilities? • What tools, processes, protocols, and strategies do you and your partners use regularly to manage the change process?	• ULs • District partner leads • State partner leads
	• Can you describe the district's roles and responsibilities in planning and implementing program changes?	• District partner leads
	• What systems, mechanisms or routines do you have in place to promote engagement of all partners, and support progress toward UPPI goals?	• UPPI leadership team
	• What have you heard about the [program] redesign? • What are your greatest concerns about the [program's] redesign or the redesign process?	• Research faculty • Adjunct faculty • Mentor principals • Principal candidates

Table C.4—continued

Research Question	Sample Questions	Respondent/Protocols
Partner engagement	• How often do you interact with the various partners? • Are there organizations or individuals missing that are essential for the program improvement effort?	• ULs • District partner leads • State partner leads • Mentor program leads
	• Is your district's engagement in the UPPI consistent with your expectations at the start of the partnership?	• District partner leads
	• Please describe the [state organization's] role in the reform of [program].	• State partner leads
	• What are some limitations to the support you are able to provide?	• Mentor program leads
Challenges and solutions	• What one or two major challenges have you encountered? • What lessons learned or advice would you offer to other universities or programs attempting similar initiatives?	• ULs • District partner leads • Mentor program leads

UPPI Leadership Team Meeting Observation

In Box C.1, we present the open-ended protocol we developed and used to guide the observation of the UPPI leadership team meetings.

Coding

All interview and focus group notes were transcribed along with team meeting observation notes and uploaded to Dedoose 7.6.21 (SocioCultural Research Consultants, 2016), a cloud-based qualitative analysis software for coding and analysis. We coded transcripts from each site visit as soon as they were available, meaning that we did two waves of coding. Each time, we began by applying descriptor codes to all documents. These codes identified the organizational affiliation of the individual making the comment and his or her role within the organization. These descriptor codes allowed us to search documents with ease and to track consistencies and discrepancies in how individuals representing different types of organizations reported on program changes and the change process.

We engaged in multiple readings and performed iterative coding, wherein preliminary coding on topics was followed by thematic coding (Creswell and Poth, 2017; Miles and Huberman, 1994; Yin, 2014, 2015). The initial set of topic codes were derived from the key constructs in the interview protocols, which, in turn, reflected the research questions, which aligned with the UPPI approach. Topic codes (and subcodes) included, for example, background and context of each organization (e.g., demographics, institutional policies and structures), partner engagement (e.g., role played, perception of engagement), management of the change process (e.g., strategies, processes, tools), program changes (e.g., curriculum content, instructional approach,

Box C.1
UPPI Leadership Team Meeting Observation Protocol

Basic Information

Site (i.e., university ID) _____

Date   _____

Start Time   _____

End Time   _____

Attendees (University) _____

(District 1) _____

(District 2) _____

(District 3) _____

(State)   _____

(Provider) _____

(Other) _____

Absent Members (Note affiliation) _____

Type of Meeting (If not regular UPPI leadership team meeting) _____

Method of Obs. (In Person/Video/Phone) _____

Observers _____

Program Changes

[Collect and attach meeting agenda to observation notes. These questions pertain to agenda items substantively related to program changes, not items pertaining to logistics or scheduling.]

1. What is the team working on with respect to UPPI-related program changes? What issues were discussed? What decisions were made? What decisions needed to be made?

2. Were all agenda items addressed by the end of the meeting? Was each agenda item given sufficient/adequate attention?

3. What challenges, if any, were explicitly identified by participants with respect to program changes (e.g., "We can't change the curriculum without state approval")? What proposed solutions, if any, did participants discuss to address identified challenges?

Change Process

4. What tools, processes, or strategies were mentioned that support the change process?

    a. How were they used?

    b. What tools, processes, or strategies were used during the meeting (e.g., a facilitation protocol, team meeting norms)?

5. What challenges arose related to the change process? How were they addressed?

Partner Engagement

6. Who facilitated the meeting?

7. How was the distribution of contributions/voices (e.g., did an individual dominate, did everyone have a chance to participate, was any individual particularly vocal or quiet, given the topics of discussion)?

8. Around what topics or decisions were there agreements/consensus? How did participants arrive at a consensus?

9. Around what topics or decisions were there disagreements or tension? How were those disagreements addressed?

Challenges

[Addressed in #3, 5, 9]

clinical experiences, LTS vision), and challenges and facilitators of various aspects of the initiative. In addition to a priori codes, we allowed for emergent coding, particularly during thematic coding (Miles and Huberman, 1994). We applied multiple codes to an excerpt as relevant.

We followed established qualitative research procedures for ensuring reliability in our coding process (Denzin and Lincoln, 2003; Lincoln and Guba, 1985; Miles and Huberman, 1994; Strauss and Corbin, 1994). Our team of four qualitative analysts and two researchers met to establish an initial coding scheme, define the codes, and train on the coding scheme. As coding progressed, we held weekly meetings to discuss and resolve ambiguities and discrepancies. As a result, we revised the coding scheme and documented decision rules as necessary. A primary analyst coded the data for each site. A secondary analyst/researcher coded a subset of transcripts (3–5 for the first wave of coding) for reliability check. The pairs of coders met to discuss and resolve discrepancies through consensus, bringing further unresolved issues to the larger research team for further discussion and final decision.

Data Analysis

Data analysis was guided by analytical questions that we developed a priori that were keyed to our four primary research questions. Analysis involved running multiple relevant queries on substantive codes of interest to answer analytical questions that correspond to the main research questions. We identified the codes to use for queries a priori and expanded them based on initial analysis. We identified themes following established techniques (Bernard, Wutich, and Ryan, 2016; Ryan and Bernard, 2003). After the spring site visit, we produced an internal memo summarizing the progress and key findings that characterized each site, which helped in understanding each site and in generating possible cross-site themes. For this report, we analyzed all data from spring and fall site visits together.

We took multiple steps to ensure the integrity of our findings. We convened after each wave of site visits to identify cross-cutting emerging themes. These meetings also provided regular opportunities to check for underlying analyst assumptions or biases (Denzin and Lincoln, 2003; Lincoln and Guba, 1985). Throughout the analysis process, we sought both confirmatory and disconfirming evidence and triangulated data across sources and time. Finally, we conducted fact-checking; we made the sections of the report that explicitly referenced specific sites available for ULs to review for accuracy.

Limitations

The data have several limitations. First, all interview and focus group data were self-reports. As such, they reflected individual perspectives and were not independently verified. Second, focus group participants, particularly supervising principals and principal candidates, were often a convenience sample. Interviews and focus group participants may not represent all possible participants' perspectives. Lastly, due to scheduling and technical limitations, we were unable to attend all UPPI leadership team meetings in person. Joining team meetings by phone or video conference may have limited our ability to observe the full range of interactions in the room.

References

Anderson, L.M., Turnbull, B. J., and Arcaira, E.R. (2017). *Leader tracking systems: Turning data into information for school leadership.* Washington, DC: Policy Studies Associates, Inc.

Bernard, H.R., Wutich, A., and Ryan, G.W. (2016). *Analyzing qualitative data: Systematic approaches.* Thousand Oaks, CA: Sage.

Bottoms, G., and O'Neill, K. (2001). *Preparing a new breed of school principals: It's time for action.* Atlanta, GA: Southern Regional Education Board.

Briggs, K., Cheney, G., Davis, J., and Moll, K. (2013). *Operating in the dark: What outdated state policies and data gaps mean for effective school leadership.* Dallas, TX: The George W. Bush Institute.

Carnegie Foundation (2017). *The Carnegie classification of institutions of higher education.* As of September 17, 2018:
http://carnegieclassifications.iu.edu/lookup/lookup.php

Creswell, J.W., and Poth, C.N. (2017). *Qualitative inquiry and research design: Choosing among five approaches.* Thousand Oaks, CA: Sage.

Darling-Hammond, L., LaPointe, M., Meyerson, D., and Orr, M.T. (2007). *Preparing school leaders for a changing world: Lessons from exemplary leadership development programs.* Stanford, CA: Stanford University. As of September 17, 2018:
http://www.wallacefoundation.org/knowledge-center/school-leadership/key-research/Documents/Preparing-School-Leaders.pdf

Daugherty, L., Herman, R., and Unlu, F. (2017). *Logic models for selecting, designing, and implementing evidence-based school leadership interventions: Companion guide to "School leadership interventions under the Every Student Succeeds Act."* Santa Monica, CA: RAND Corporation, TL-274-WF. As of September 17, 2018:
https://www.rand.org/pubs/tools/TL274.html

Davis, J. (2016). *Improving university principal preparation programs: Five themes from the field.* New York, NY: The Wallace Foundation.

Denzin, N.K., and Lincoln, Y.S. (2003). The discipline and practice of qualitative research. In N.K. Denzin and Y.S. Lincoln (eds.). *Collecting and interpreting qualitative materials* (2nd ed., pp. 1–45). Thousand Oaks, CA: Sage.

DuFour, R. (2004). What is a "professional learning community"? *Educational Leadership, 61*(8), 6–11.

Education Development Center (2009, 2018). *Quality Measures, Tenth Edition.* As of September 17, 2018:
http://www.wallacefoundation.org/knowledge-center/Documents/Principal-Preparation-Program-Quality-Self-Assessment-Rubrics.pdf

Fry, B., Bottoms, G., and O'Neill, K. (2005). *The principal internship: How can we get it right?* Atlanta, GA: Southern Regional Education Board. As of September 17, 2018: https://www.sreb.org/publication/principal-internship-0

Gates, S.M., Ringel, J.S., Santibanez, L., Chung, C.H., and Ross, K.E. (2003). *Who is leading our schools? An overview of school administrators and their careers.* Santa Monica, CA: RAND Corporation. MR-1679-EDU. As of September 17, 2018: https://www.rand.org/pubs/monograph_reports/MR1679.html

Gill, J. (2016). *Chock full of data: How school districts are building leader tracking systems to support principal pipelines. Stories from the field.* New York, NY: The Wallace Foundation.

Grissom, J.A., and Loeb, S. (2011). Triangulating principal effectiveness: How perspectives of parents, teachers, and assistant principals identify the central importance of managerial skills. *American Educational Research Journal, 48*(5), 1091–1123.

Hale, E.L., and Moorman, H.N. (2003). *Preparing school principals: A national perspective on policy and program innovations.* Washington, DC: Institute for Educational Leadership, and Edwardsville, IL: Illinois Education Research Council.

Harvey, J., and Holland, H. (2013). *The school principal as leader: Guiding schools to better teaching and learning (Expanded edition).* New York, NY: The Wallace Foundation.

Herman, R., Gates, S.M., Arifkhanova, A., Bega, A., Chavez-Herreias, E.R., Han, E., Harris, M., Leschitz, J., and Wrabel, S.L. (2017). *School leadership interventions under the Every Student Succeeds Act: Evidence review.* Santa Monica, CA: RAND Corporation. RR-1550-3-WF. As of September 14, 2018: https://www.rand.org/pubs/research_reports/RR1550-3.html

Hess, F.M. and Kelly, A.P. (2007). *Learning to lead? What gets taught in principal preparation programs. Teachers College Record, 109*(1), 244–274. As of September 14, 2018: https://sites.hks.harvard.edu/pepg/PDF/Papers/Hess_Kelly_Learning_to_Lead_PEPG05.02.pdf

Holmes Group (1990). *Tomorrow's schools: Principles for the design of professional development schools: Executive summary.* East Lansing, MI.

Holmes Group (1995). *Tomorrow's schools of education: A report of the Holmes Group.* East Lansing, MI.

Hudson, R. (2016). *Creating university/K–12 partnerships for the enhancement of educational leadership preparation and increasing student achievement: Sustainability factors, barriers, and benefits* (doctoral dissertation). Auburn, AL: Auburn University.

Kaufman, J.H., Gates, S.M., Harvey, M., Wang, Y., and Barrett, M. (2017). *What it takes to operate and maintain principal pipelines.* Santa Monica, CA: RAND Corporation. RR-2078-WF. As of September 14, 2018: https://www.rand.org/pubs/research_reports/RR2078.html

Knapp, M.S., Copland, M.A., Honig, M.I., Plecki, M.L., and Portin, B.S. (2010). *Learning-focused leadership and leadership support: Meaning and practice in urban systems.* Seattle, WA: Center for the Study of Teaching and Policy–University of Washington.

Larsen, E., Clifford, M., Lemke, M., Chambers, D., Swanlund, A. (2016a). *Following the leaders: An analysis of graduate effectiveness from five principal preparation programs.* Dallas, TX: The George W. Bush Institute.

Larsen, E., Clifford, M., Lemke, M., Chambers, D., Swanlund, A. (2016b). *Developing Leaders: The importance—and the challenges—of evaluating principal preparation programs.* Dallas, TX: The George W. Bush Institute.

Levine, A. (2005). *Educating school leaders.* New York, NY: Teachers College, The Education Schools Project.

Lincoln, Y.S., and Guba, E.G. (1985). *Naturalistic inquiry.* Beverly Hills, CA: Sage.

Louis, K.S., Leithwood, K., Wahlstrom, K., and Anderson, S. (2010). *Learning from leadership: Investigating the links to improved student learning.* New York, NY: The Wallace Foundation.

Manna, P. (2015). *Developing excellent school principals to advance teaching and learning: Considerations for state policy.* New York, NY: The Wallace Foundation.

McDiarmid, G.W., and Caprino, K. (2017). *Lessons from the Teachers for a New Era project: Evidence and accountability in teacher education.* New York, NY: Routledge.

Miles, M.B., and Huberman, A.M. (1994). *Qualitative data analysis: An expanded sourcebook.* Thousand Oaks, CA: Sage.

National Policy Board for Educational Administration (2015). *Professional Standards for Educational Leaders 2015.* Reston, VA.

NPBEA—*See* National Policy Board for Educational Administration.

Phillips, J.C. (2013). State mandated principal preparation program redesign: Impetus for reform or invitation to chaos? *Journal of Research on Leadership Education, 8*(2), 139–151.

Public Law 89-10 (April 11, 1965). Elementary and Secondary Education Act.

Public Law 114-95 (December 10, 2015). Every Student Succeeds Act.

Ryan, G.W., and Bernard, H.R. (2003). Techniques to identify themes. *Field Methods, 15*(1), 85–109.

Sherman, W., and Cunningham, W. (2006). *Improving administrative preparation and practice through well-designed internships.* Paper presented at the 2006 University Council for Educational Administration Annual Conference, San Antonio, TX.

SocioCultural Research Consultants, LLC (2016). Dedoose Version 7.6.21. *Dedoose web application for managing, analyzing, and presenting qualitative and mixed method research data.* Los Angeles, CA. As of September 17, 2018:
http://www.dedoose.com

Stallings, J.A., Wiseman, D.L., and Knight, S.L. (1995). Professional development schools: A new generation of school-university partnerships in Petrie, H. G. (ed.). *Professionalization, partnership, and power: Building professional development schools.* New York, NY: State University of New York Press.

Strauss, A., and Corbin, J. (1994). Grounded theory methodology. *Handbook of Qualitative Research, 17,* 273–85.

University Council for Educational Administration (2018). Draft National Educational Leadership Preparation standards. As of October 1, 2018:
http://www.ucea.org/initiatives/1523/

University of Wisconsin Extension School (2002). *Enhancing program performance with logic models.* [Course.] Madison, WI: Author.

U.S. Department of Education (2017a). *Institute of Education Sciences, National Center for Education Statistics.* Washington, DC.

U.S. Department of Education, Office for Civil Rights (2017b). *Civil Rights Data Collection, 2013–2014.* Washington, DC.

Wilmore, E.L., and Bratlien M.J. (2005). Mentoring and tutoring within administrative internship programs in American universities, *Mentoring and Tutoring: Partnership in Learning, 13*(1), 23–37.

W.K. Kellogg Foundation (1998). *Foundation evaluation handbook*. East Battle Creek, MI.

Yin, R.K. (2014). *Case study research: Design and methods*. Thousand Oaks, CA: Sage.

Yin, R.K. (2015). *Qualitative research from start to finish*. New York, NY: Guilford Publications.